Easy Programming
with QBasic™

Tory Stephen Toupin

Easy Programming with QBasic™

Copyright © 1994 by Que® Corporation.

Library of Congress Catalog No.: 94-67594

ISBN: 1-56529-995-7

96 95 94   6 5 4 3 2 1

Interpretation of the printing code: the rightmost double-digit number is the year of the book's printing; the rightmost single-digit number, the number of the book's printing. For example, a printing code of 94-1 shows that the first printing of the book occurred in 1994.

Publisher: David P. Ewing

Associate Publisher: Joseph B. Wikert

Publishing Manager: Steven M. Schafer

Product Marketing Manager: Greg Wiegand

Credits

Title Manager
Bryan Gambrel

Acquisitions Editor
Fred Slone

Production Editors
Linda Seifert
Mike La Bonne

Technical Editor
Brian Stanek
Michael Watson

Acquisitions Coordinator
Patricia Brooks

Book Designer
Amy Peppler-Adams

Cover Designer
Jay Corpus

Graphic Image Specialists
Becky Beheler
Jason Hand
Clint Lahnen
Dennis Sheehan
Craig Small

Production Team
Stephen Adams
Cameron Booker
Stephen Carlin
Anne Dickerson
Rich Evers
Caroline Roop
Nanci Sears Perry
Kris Simmons
Tina Trettin

Indexer
Michael Hughes

Composed in *Stone Serif* and *MCPdigital* by Que Corporation

About the Author

Tory Stephen Toupin has been programming for the past nine years in real estate, industrial control, finance, and educational arenas. His primary areas of research include artificial intelligence, distributed application development, object-oriented development, and simulation and modeling. He graduated summa cum laude from the University of Denver in Mathematics and Computer Science and is a lifetime member of Phi Beta Kappa. Tory developed real time process control application utilities for a Denver-based oil company and is working in Switzerland at the Swiss Scientific Computing Center in high-performance language tools for parallel scientific computing. Tory is an avid jogger and organist.

Trademark Acknowledgments

All terms mentioned in this book that are known to be trademarks or service marks have been appropriately capitalized. Que Corporation cannot attest to the accuracy of this information. Use of a term in this book should not be regarded as affecting the validity of any trademark or service mark.

Contents at a Glance

Introduction 1

Part 1: Elements of a QBasic Program 4

Part 2: Data Types, Constants, and Variables 18

Part 3: Basic Input and Output 36

Part 4: Decisions, Repetition, and Control 56

Part 5: Subroutines, Procedures, and Functions 78

Part 6: Mathematics 94

Part 7: Strings and String Manipulation 116

Part 8: Sound and Graphics 130

Part 9: Sequential File Input and Output 148

Part 10: Random-Access File Input and Output 162

Index 176

Contents

Introduction   1

Part 1: Elements of a QBasic Program   4

1	Element Soup	8
2	Constants and Variables	10
3	Statements	12
4	Operators	14
5	Functions and Procedures	16

Part 2: Data Types, Constants, and Variables   18

6	A Variable by Any Other Name	22
7	Giving Variables a Value	24
8	To Be Precise	26
9	Whole Numbers	28
10	Character Strings	30
11	Arrays and Tables	32
12	New Structures from Old	34

Part 3: Basic Input and Output   36

13	Input from the Keyboard	40
14	Output to the Screen	42
15	Formatted Output	44
16	Columns Like You Want Them	46
17	Waiting for that Special Key	48
18	Getting Data Directly from Your Program	50
19	Looking for DATA	52
20	Sending Output to a Printer	54

Part 4: Decisions, Repetition, and Control　56

21　Unconditional Branching 60
22　Branch by Number..62
23　Boolean Algebra and Boolean Expressions 64
24　Conditional Branching 66
25　More Conditional Execution 68
26　Case by Case...70
27　Looping 72
28　WHILE...WEND and DO...LOOP 74
29　Jumping Out of the System...76

Part 5: Subroutines, Procedures, and Functions　78

30　Subroutines that Come Back..82
31　Branch by Number..84
32　Subroutines...86
33　Functions..88
34　Longer Functions 90
35　Subroutines that Give Something Back 92

Part 6: Mathematics　94

36　Setting a Precedent...98
37　More or Less Mathematics 100
38　Multiplication 102
39　Fun with Fractions 104
40　Giving the Computer the Third Degree..106
41　A Reminder...Remainder...108
42　Rounding...110
43　Random Number Generation RND...112
44　Seeing the Signs...114

Part 7: Strings and String Manipulation   116

45   Simple String Building 120
46   Searching for Substrings in a String..122
47   Character Codes and Numeric Strings..124
48   Do You Have the Time? 126
49   More String-Building Functions...128

Part 8: Sound and Graphics   130

50   Sound Off! 134
51   Making Music 136
52   Getting into Graphics 138
53   Plotting Points...140
54   Geometric Figures 142
55   Filling Figures 144
56   Turtle Graphics..146

Part 9: Sequential File Input and Output   148

57   Setting Up Your Files..152
58   Storing Data in a File..154
59   Retrieving Data from a File 156
60   Delimiting Data..158
61   Checking for the End..160

Part 10: Random-Access File Input and Output 162

62   Setting Up Your Files..166
63   Describing Records...168
64   Storing Records..170
65   Retrieving Records...172
66   Positioning within the File 174

Index   176

Introduction

Congratulations! You have just opened the door to the wonderful world of computer programming! This book is an introduction to programming with the QBasic interpreter that comes with MS-DOS 5.0 or later. If you have never programmed a computer before, but have thought about the many things you want your computer to do for you, this is the place to start!

The History of BASIC— A Short Version

QBasic supports the BASIC programming language. BASIC stands for *Beginners All-Purpose Symbolic Instruction Code* and was initially designed in 1963 by John Kemeny and Thomas Kurtz to support the educational needs of nonscience students. BASIC was a revolutionary language for the time. BASIC is easy to learn and understand, and the programs you will learn to write are easy to translate from English because the way BASIC expresses things is very much like English commands: INPUT some information, PRINT some results, GOTO some place in the program, and so on.

QBasic

The BASIC language comes in many forms. QBasic is what is called a BASIC *interpreter*. QBasic lets you enter programs into the editor then start, or run, them. QBasic looks through your program one step at a time, doing exactly what your program tells it to do. QBasic serves as an intermediary between your program and the computer: your program tells QBasic to do something, then QBasic makes the computer take the right action.

Interpreters like QBasic are wonderful for learning how to program. You can make changes to your program quickly, sometimes even while the program is running. This makes experimenting with the BASIC language exciting because you can try out your ideas and get immediate response.

Limits of QBasic

QBasic is an excellent place for you to start to learn computer programming. QBasic has some limitations, but you won't need to worry about these while you are learning.

So, take a seat at your computer, start QBasic, and get ready to have some fun! Be warned, though: after you start programming, you will inevitably spend many joyful but sleepless nights experimenting with your computer through the BASIC language!

Who This Book Is For

This book is for people who want to learn how to program their computer with QBasic. More importantly, this book is for people who have flipped through other programming texts only to be discouraged by a foreign language and verbose explanations that lead them to drift off to never-never land. *Easy Programming with QBasic* uses a conversational style in the explanations and shows short programming examples. Together, these elements take you right into the QBasic language without any fear of getting lost in the jargon jungle.

Each lesson contains a short QBasic language code segment. You can run these programs on your computer as you work your way through the book.

Due to space limitations in this book, we sometimes had to break code lines in illegal spots. To indicate two lines of code that must be typed on a single line, we have used a red arrow (↵).

Each code segment is broken down into numbered steps, which are then explained line by line.

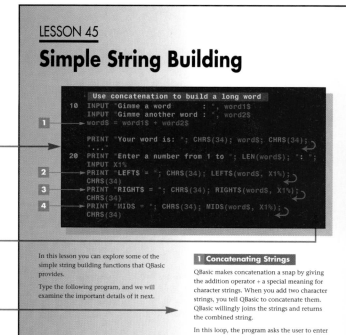

LESSON 45
Simple String Building

```
     Use concatenation to build a long word
10   INPUT "Gimme a word        : ", word1$
     INPUT "Gimme another word : ", word2$
1    word$ = word1$ + word2$

     PRINT "Your word is: "; CHR$(34); word$; CHR$(34);
     "..."
20   PRINT "Enter a number from 1 to "; LEN(word$); ": ";
     INPUT X1%
2    PRINT "LEFT$ = "; CHR$(34); LEFT$(word$, X1%);
     CHR$(34)
3    PRINT "RIGHT$ = "; CHR$(34); RIGHT$(word$, X1%);
     CHR$(34)
4    PRINT "MID$ = "; CHR$(34); MID$(word$, X1%);
     CHR$(34)
```

In this lesson you can explore some of the simple string building functions that QBasic provides.

Type the following program, and we will examine the important details of it next.

1 Concatenating Strings

QBasic makes concatenation a snap by giving the addition operator + a special meaning for character strings. When you add two character strings, you tell QBasic to concatenate them. QBasic willingly joins the strings and returns the combined string.

In this loop, the program asks the user to enter a word. The first word is stored in word1$ while the second is stored in word2$. Both variables are then concatenated and stored into the variable word$.

120

2

Because its focus is on beginning programmers, *Easy Programming with QBasic* is not a complete QBasic programming reference—and therefore doesn't attempt to provide a comprehensive explanation into the techniques of professional programming. It merely provides you with a quick taste of QBasic programming to pique your interest in programming. After reading this book, you will have a solid understanding of QBasic programming fundamentals; you will be ready to move on to those more verbose texts and begin writing many useful and rewarding programs.

A Sample Lesson

This book is divided into 10 parts. Each part is then divided into several lessons. Each lesson is two pages containing a short code segment and a brief discussion of that code, line by line. Throughout this book, you will notice that I use a color scheme that makes each type of QBasic word, similar to the parts of speech in a language, a different color.

Here is a breakdown of one of these lessons.

In each lesson, you get a brief summary of each line of code, followed by a thorough explanation of what that line does, and how to use it in a program. Throughout the book, QBasic terms appear in the same color scheme used in the program segments.

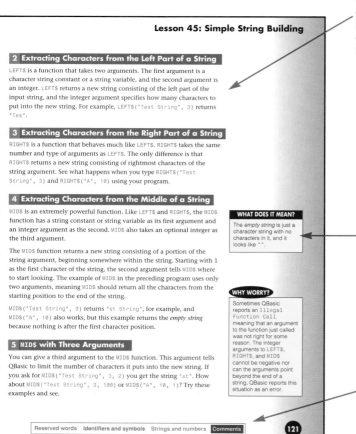

Lesson 45: Simple String Building

2 Extracting Characters from the Left Part of a String

LEFT$ is a function that takes two arguments. The first argument is a character string constant or a string variable, and the second argument is an integer. LEFT$ returns a new string consisting of the left part of the input string, and the integer argument specifies how many characters to put into the new string. For example, LEFT$("Test String", 3) returns "Tes".

3 Extracting Characters from the Right Part of a String

RIGHT$ is a function that behaves much like LEFT$. RIGHT$ takes the same number and type of arguments as LEFT$. The only difference is that RIGHT$ returns a new string consisting of rightmost characters of the string argument. See what happens when you type RIGHT$("Test String", 3) and RIGHT$("A", 10) using your program.

4 Extracting Characters from the Middle of a String

MID$ is an extremely powerful function. Like LEFT$ and RIGHT$, the MID$ function has a string constant or string variable as its first argument and an integer argument as the second. MID$ also takes an optional integer as the third argument.

The MID$ function returns a new string consisting of a portion of the string argument, beginning somewhere within the string. Starting with 1 as the first character of the string, the second argument tells MID$ where to start looking. The example of MID$ in the preceding program uses only two arguments, meaning MID$ should return all the characters from the starting position to the end of the string.

MID$("Test String", 3) returns "st String", for example, and MID$("A", 10) also works, but this example returns the *empty string* because nothing is after the first character position.

WHAT DOES IT MEAN?

The *empty string* is just a character string with no characters in it, and it looks like "".

5 MID$ with Three Arguments

You can give a third argument to the MID$ function. This argument tells QBasic to limit the number of characters it puts into the new string. If you ask for MID$("Test String", 3, 2) you get the string "st". How about MID$("Test String", 3, 100) or MID$("A", 10, 1)? Try these examples and see.

WHY WORRY?

Sometimes QBasic reports an Illegal Function Call, meaning that an argument to the function just called was not right for some reason. The integer arguments to LEFT$, RIGHT$, and MID$ cannot be negative nor can the arguments point beyond the end of a string. QBasic reports this situation as an error.

Reserved words   Identifiers and symbols   Strings and numbers   Comments

121

Throughout this book, you will find small boxes of text, labelled "Note," "What Does It Mean?," and "Why Worry?" These boxes contain information, definitions, and hints from the author that will help you through rough spots. New terms and emphasized words are presented in *italicized* text; pay close attention

At the bottom of every lesson is a color-key that explains the colors used for the QBasic terms. In each program listing and in the text of the lesson, QBasic reserved words are green, identifiers and symbols are red, strings and numbers are gray, and comments are yellow with a purple background. This same color scheme is used throughout the entire book.

BASIC

```
Dim x As Currency
x=500
    •
    •
    •
    •
Print "$";x
```

PART 1

Elements of a QBasic Program

Writing programs in QBasic is really a snap. There are only a few basic elements that make up the programs you write, and putting these together requires just a bit of imagination and an idea that you want to implement.

What Is a Program?

QBasic programs consist of lines of commands that instruct QBasic to make your computer take some action. In fact, programs are very much like recipes! QBasic takes a program that you write and looks at each line in succession, performing the action you tell it.

The commands that direct QBasic to take action are called *statements*. Like commands in English, QBasic statements take objects of action, called *arguments*. The PRINT statement in QBasic causes information to be displayed on the screen. For QBasic to know what information to display, you must supply arguments.

WHAT DOES IT MEAN?

Statements are words you use in your programs that direct QBasic to take some action, such as printing information on the screen (PRINT) or getting information from the user (INPUT). Statements act on objects you specify. These objects, called *arguments*, tell QBasic what to print or where to store the information it gets from the user.

Arguments come in many different flavors, depending on what kind of information you want to keep. The type of information is called

1 Element Soup

2 Constants and Variables

3 Statements

4 Operators

5 Functions and Procedures

the *data type*, and QBasic has five major data types: four for numbers, and one for text and other information.

Although having four different kinds of numbers may seem overwhelming, the distinction is easy to understand. Each number your program uses must be stored somewhere in memory. Because only so much memory is available, QBasic sets aside a small, fixed amount of memory to store each kind of number. By limiting the amount of space available to store the numbers, QBasic also limits the range and precision of numbers it can store. Consider the amount blank on your personal checks. In most cases, this blank is only one inch wide, so the amount you write on a personal check is limited to however many digits you can scribble in there!

You don't have much choice as to how wide the amount blank is on your checks, but QBasic gives you some degree of freedom on this subject by letting you choose how wide the "blanks," or variables, should be in your program with these four numeric data types. Each numeric data type has a different range and precision. It is up to you to choose the data type that suits your needs.

Constants and Variables

Besides the data type, arguments are either constant, such as 7 or 1000.502, or variable. Constants are entities that can never change their value. The example of 7 is constant because its value is always 7. *Variables*, however, are entities that hold data temporarily and can change their contents while your program runs. This is what gives your programs the ability to process information and generate usable results. Data that is being processed is held temporarily in

variables. Variables hold intermediate calculations and, ultimately, the final results on which your program is working.

Think about the balance in your checking account. It can help to look at your check register. The account balance is a variable. At any moment, you can find the account balance, but this number changes with each check you write or deposit you make.

Program Flow

When QBasic executes a program, it starts at the first line in the program and continues to the last. But programs that always take one path from beginning to end probably don't do much! For a program to properly process information supplied by the user, it must make decisions and change paths occasionally. These path changes are called *program flow changes*, and QBasic has many ways to do this with *flow control statements*.

WHAT DOES IT MEAN?

Flow control statements tell QBasic to execute some part of your program that is not in the natural top-to-bottom flow of the program. Flow control statements include statements for repeating a part of your program several times (loops), statements for executing a part of your program only under certain conditions (conditional execution), and statements for using a common part of your program throughout its execution (subroutines).

Programs in QBasic have special markers called *line numbers* and *line labels* that act like bookmarks. When your program makes a decision, it tells QBasic, "If *this* is true, then turn to *that* page and do what it says there; otherwise, keep reading from here."

When QBasic changes paths, it forgets about the decision that caused it to change.

It simply goes on with the statements that the line number or line label indicate. Sometimes, though, your program needs QBasic to execute a part of your program, then come back and continue where it left off.

Subroutines are portions of your program that are given a name and can be used by other parts of the program. Suppose that you want to try an advanced recipe on Cajun cooking for alligator sauce picante. The recipe calls for a tomato roux and refers you to page 6. Page 6 tells you how to make this tomato roux, but it needs a basic roux itself! So, turn to page 3, make the basic roux, and when that is finished, turn back to the recipe for the tomato roux, make that, and finally return to the alligator sauce picante recipe.

The reason for all that page flipping was to save space and reduce errors in the cookbook. Tomato roux and basic roux are common to many recipes in the cookbook. If you make changes to the recipe for roux, you don't need to change it in every recipe; it is changed only once. More important, the recipe for the sauce is much easier to understand: rather than combining the recipes for the roux and the sauce, this recipe needs to contain directions only for the sauce.

Subroutines (or procedures) work similarly in your programs. You can break your programs up into common procedures. Every time you need to carry out a particular procedure, you tell QBasic which procedure to perform. After QBasic has executed that procedure, it returns to where you called that procedure, and your program continues running.

Internal Documentation

One of the most important parts of any program is actually completely ignored by QBasic: the program comments. *Comments* are text that describe what the program is doing. When you look at a program written by someone else, it is often difficult to figure out just by reading the program statements. Sometimes, it is even hard to remember what you are doing in your own programs! QBasic has a couple of ways to put comments in your program—and they are simple enough that you have no excuse not to put comments in your code.

But comments are only one way to explain to readers what your program is doing. Comments are part of your program's *internal documentation*, which consists of all hints that readers can use to follow your programs. Internal documentation includes line labels, descriptive constant and variable names, subroutines and procedures, and comments. In fact, just using the right name for a variable or subroutine can take the place of many comments.

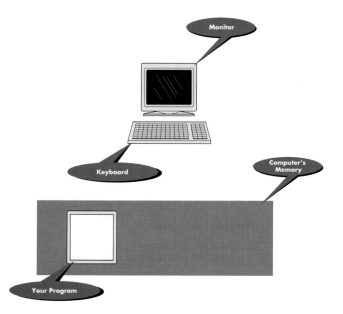

LESSON 1

Element Soup

```
1    REM This is a comment
2    REM You should comment your code with useful
     ' comments that give a general idea of what
5    ' your program is doing
3    10        X = 1024.05   ' Put an initial value in X
4    Print.The.Value:
6         PRINT X + 5
7         GOTO 10
```

A QBasic program is composed of just a few fundamental parts. Read over the program, read the explanations, then type the program. After you run the program, press Ctrl-Break to get back to QBasic. Don't be concerned with the real details to this program. You will understand this program before you have finished this book.

1 Comments

Comments are an important but optional part of any program. Comments let you explain what certain parts of your program are doing. Even if you are the only person writing a program, comments can be extremely valuable. If you leave a program alone for even a day, comments can help you restore your train of thought.

QBasic has two ways to put comments in your programs. One way is with the REM statement (short for REMark). QBasic ignores anything on a line after the REM statement.

WHY WORRY?

The REM statement must appear on a line by itself. QBasic gives you a Syntax Error if you try putting a remark on the same line as another statement with the REM statement. You can use the apostrophe (') if you want to put comments at the end of a statement.

2 The Apostrophe

The second way of putting comments in your programs is to use the apostrophe ('). The apostrophe is more useful than REM because you can place a remark with the apostrophe on the same line as another QBasic statement.

3 Line Numbers

Line numbers are numbers that mark special places in your program. Line numbers must be positive whole numbers like 5 or 10500, and they have to appear at the beginning of the line. As long as you don't use the same line number more than once, you can put line numbers in any order you want. You will see how to use line numbers in Part 4, "Decisions, Repetition, and Control."

4 Line Labels

Line labels mark special places in your program. Line labels are more descriptive than line numbers.

5 Identifiers

An identifier is a name that you use to distinguish variables in QBasic. Variables are objects in QBasic that can change their value as your program runs.

6 Keywords

You cannot really use every possible identifier for your own programs. QBasic reserves some identifiers, called *keywords*, for special purposes. Keywords make up the statements that QBasic uses to control your computer, such as PRINT, which displays information on the screen. Because QBasic reserves PRINT, you cannot use it as an identifier in your programs. You recognize the keywords by their color in this book.

7 Symbols

Symbols, colored red in this book, are special characters that tell QBasic to take some action. QBasic does mathematics with the mathematical symbols +, -, *, / and many others. There are many symbols that QBasic uses, and you encounter these as you learn QBasic.

NOTE

Line numbers get special treatment by QBasic. Line numbers can be any sequence containing up to 40 digits. If the line number is not more than 65530, leading zeroes are ignored. This means that line numbers 65530 and 065530 are the same. In fact, the QBasic editor will change 065530 to 65530 if you use it as a line number. However, the line numbers 65531, 065531 and 0065531 are thought of as different line numbers by QBasic.

WHY WORRY?

An identifier can be a sequence of up to 40 alphabetic characters. Actually, besides characters, identifiers can contain numbers or the period (.), as long as the identifier begins with an alphabetic character like a or z. An.Identifier.For.1 0.Things is a valid identifier, but 5.Names and .Ten are not acceptable. Identifiers are colored red in this book, although you won't see these colors in the editor as you type your programs.

LESSON 2

Constants and Variables

```
' Introducing...  Constants and variables!
X = 2.99
Y = X + 19.95

Pi = 314159265D-8
Pie = 42
PRINT Pi, X, Y

LargeNumber# = 1D+308

' Stringing you along...
SomeString$ = "This is a string constant with
exactly sixty-six characters in it!"
PRINT SomeString$
```

Constants are numbers your program uses for things that never change. You can keep the sales tax rate or minimum allowed balance of an account as a constant in your program. *Variables*, however, are the work areas of your program because their values change as your program is running. You use variables to store information and calculations temporarily.

This program has several examples of variables and constants. Part 2, "Data Types, Constants, and Variables," covers these in more detail.

1 Identifiers

As shown in Lesson 1, identifiers can be used for several things, but their most common use is for naming variables.

Each variable name represents a different variable. You can think of variable names as bank account numbers. Each bank account number, or account identifier, represents a balance in a distinct account. One account identifier always refers to the same account, even though the balance might change. Variable names, like X and Y, behave similarly. X and Y represent two different variables. But X always refers to the same variable throughout the program, even though its contents might change. The same is true for Y.

NOTE

Due to space limitations in this book, we sometimes had to break code lines in illegal spots. To indicate two lines of code that must be typed on a single line, we have used a red arrow (↵).

2 Assignment Statements

Variables hold data temporarily. The way you get information into variables is with an *assignment statement*. You can store many different things in a variable, including the data from other variables (expressions like X + 19.95) and constants.

3 Constants

Constants are unchanging data that are part of your program. QBasic has two kinds of constants: numeric constants and string constants. You probably use numeric constants during most of your day, like $2.99, $19.95, or $5,999.99. However, QBasic does not understand numbers with special characters like the comma (,) or dollar sign ($). A numeric constant must be a sequence of digits only, with a possible fractional part preceded by a period. Numeric constants also can have an optional sign, such as -51.50 or +209.54.

4 Scientific Notation

To express very large or very small numbers, QBasic enables you to give constants in scientific notation. You can tell QBasic to use scientific notation by tacking on a D or an E followed by a whole number to the end of the constant. The whole number following the D or E tells QBasic how many places right (or left, if the number is negative) to shift the decimal point. The constant 314159265D-8 is the same as the constant 3.14159265#, for example. You can use scientific notation wherever you like, but it is most useful for writing large or small numbers. Try writing 5D+307!

5 Overflow

Try changing this line so that the constant is 1.9D+308. QBasic gives you an Overflow error. QBasic only allocates so much space for variables and constants. Therefore, variables and constants can only have a limited range.

6 String Constants

String constants are completely different than numeric constants. String constants contain text, numbers, or anything you want, enclosed between a pair of double quotation marks (" ").

WHY WORRY?

The QBasic editor sometimes makes small changes to what you type. When you type the sample program for this lesson into the editor, it automatically changes the constant 314159265D-8 to 3.14159265#. Both numbers have the same value, but QBasic keeps only the shortest, most accurate representation.

WHY WORRY?

You cannot, however, put a quotation mark within a string constant! Something like "double quotes " are nice" would confuse QBasic. QBasic does have a way to insert a quotation mark within a string, as well as many other tools for handling strings. You will learn about these tools in Part 7, "Strings and String Manipulation."

LESSON 3

Statements

```
         ' Get name and age
Start:        PRINT "Hi there!   ";                          1
    INPUT "What is your name"; Your.Name$
2   PRINT "Pleased to meet you, "; Your.Name$;
        ". What is your age";
    INPUT Your.Age%

        ' Check for a valid age
3   IF Your.Age% < 1 THEN GOTO Start

        ' Say something nice
    IF Your.Age% < 6 THEN
        PRINT "Well, hello there, "; Your.Name$;
            "!  Wanna learn to type?"
        INPUT Wanna.Type$
    ELSE
        PRINT "So, "; Your.Name$; ", ";
        INPUT "what can I do for you today";
            Your.Request$
    END IF

    PRINT "That's all for now, "; Your.Name$; "..."
```

Statements are the part of your programs that make QBasic do something. In fact, statements read very much like English commands. This lesson shows some examples of statements that you learn in this book. Type in this program to begin.

1 Statements

Statements command QBasic to do something. PRINT and INPUT are statements that enable you to interact with the user: PRINT displays information; INPUT gets information. Nearly every line that you put in your program looks very much like these: an optional line number, a statement, and the arguments.

2 Arguments

Arguments give statements additional directions. With the `PRINT` statement, for example, you give arguments that tell QBasic what you want to display on-screen. Arguments are generally separated by commas, but there are some special cases, like the `PRINT` statement.

3 Statements with Several Parts

Some statements take several keywords to complete the command. With the `IF...THEN` conditional execution statement, for example, the first part is the `IF` statement, followed by a condition. After the condition comes the keyword `THEN` and another statement immediately after it. Without the `THEN` keyword, QBasic would not be able to understand this line of the program.

4 Block Statements

Some statements have a *block* style. These statements have an opening statement and a closing statement (usually the `END` statement followed by the type of block). For example, the `IF...THEN` conditional execution statement also has a block style that begins with an `IF-condition-THEN` and ends with an `END IF`. The program lines between the start and end of the block contain more program statements.

> **WHAT DOES IT MEAN?**
>
> The `PRINT` statement gives you control over the spacing of the items you display on-screen. Arguments to `PRINT` can be separated by commas (`,`) or semicolons (`;`). When a semicolon separates two arguments, they are displayed immediately next to one another on-screen. Commas allow you to separate displayed arguments into columns. The peculiarities of the `PRINT` statement are covered in Part 3.

LESSON 4

Operators

```
' Operator.  Number please!
    X = 5
    Y = 7
    PRINT X + Y
' Comparison Operators
    IF X < Y THEN PRINT "Yes!  X is less than Y!"
' Logical Operators
    IF X < Y OR X > Y THEN PRINT "Well, X is
         certainly not equal to Y!"
' Precedence
    IF 3 + 5 = 7 AND "truth" <> "beauty"
         THEN PRINT "What an odd world..."
    PRINT 3 + 5 * 7
    PRINT (3 + 5) * 7
```

1
2
3
4
5
6

Operators are special characters that are used to make QBasic compute something. Like statements, operators make QBasic take some action; however, operators must be part of a statement in order to work properly.

The next program introduces several operators that you will learn about in later lessons. Look through the program to see the difference between operators and statements. Be sure to type in the program.

1 Mathematical Operators

Many of the operators that QBasic has are used for mathematical calculations, such as +, -, * and / (addition, subtraction, multiplication, and division). These operators are the *mathematical operators*.

2 Comparison Operators

Comparison operators test a relationship between two values. QBasic uses the special symbols =, <>, <, >, <=, and >= to test equal, not equal, less than, greater than, less than or equal, and greater than or equal, respectively. These operators are associated with the logical operators.

3 Logical Operators

Logical operators (such as AND, OR, or NOT) enable you to connect two or more comparisons into complicated conditions. Conditions are how you let your programs make decisions about information.

14

4 Expressions

An *expression* is a sequence of operators and the operands on which they act. For example, `3 + 5 = 7 AND "truth" <> "beauty"` is an expression. QBasic has special rules for interpreting expressions so you always know how it comes up with the answer. QBasic always evaluates expressions from left to right, as they are written. But some operators have been given higher *precedence* than others.

5 Precedence

When one operator, like `*`, has higher precedence than some other operator, say `+`, QBasic evaluates the operator with the higher precedence first. Precedence is important for QBasic in cases like `3 + 5 * 7`. Is this 56 or 38? QBasic tells you 38 because it does the multiplication first. All operators have a precedence: mathematical operators are higher than comparison operators, and comparison operators are higher than logical operators.

Operator Precedence

The precedence of all QBasic operators is given in the following table. The operators toward the top of the table have higher precedence than the operators below them and therefore get evaluated before the others. Some operators have equal precedence. These are listed at the same level of the table.

Highest	`^`
	`* /`
	`+ -`
	`< > = <> <= >=`
	`NOT`
Lowest	`AND OR`

---

6 Parentheses

Parentheses are operators designed to change the normal precedence rules. If you want some part of an expression to be evaluated as a whole, you can enclose that part in parentheses, such as `(3 + 5) * 7`.

Reserved words   Identifiers and symbols   Strings and numbers   Comments

Functions and Procedures

```
1 ──────►' Get a number and print it out
        ─►DisplayNumber

2 ──────► SUB DisplayNumber
 GetNum: ─► INPUT "Enter a number from 1 to 5: ", Num%
          ─► IF Num% < 1 OR Num% > 5 THEN GOTO GetNum
3 ─────────► PRINT "This is "; Number$(Num%)
        END SUB

5 ──────► FUNCTION Number$(I%)                          ◄────── 6
              IF I% = 1 THEN Number$ = "one"
              IF I% = 2 THEN Number$ = "two"
              IF I% = 3 THEN Number$ = "three"          ◄────── 7
              IF I% = 4 THEN Number$ = "four"
              IF I% = 5 THEN Number$ = "five"
        END FUNCTION
```

Functions and procedures are two ways you can add features QBasic does not already have. When you create procedures and functions, you can use them again and again throughout your program, just like the built-in statements of QBasic.

The next program has an example of a function and a procedure. Read all the steps before you type in this program.

1 The Main Procedure

The program you enter has a main procedure. This is where QBasic starts when you run your program.

2 Starting a Subprocedure

Procedures and functions are block statements. To enter a procedure, or subroutine, enter the starting SUB statement followed by the procedure name, which can be any identifier. As soon as you press Enter, the screen clears and you see the starting line followed by END SUB.

3 The Body of a Procedure

After the SUB statement, enter the statements that define what the procedure does. This procedure asks for a number between 1 and 5 and prints the number out as text.

4 Returning to the Main Procedure

To get back to the main procedure, press F2. This brings up a window with the name of your program and the name of the procedure indented on the next line. To return to the main procedure, use the cursor keys to move to the top, and press Enter.

5 Starting a Function

A function is very much like a procedure except that it returns a value to the main program. The addition operator (+) is an example of a function: it adds two values and returns their sum. Functions begin much the same way as procedures: enter the FUNCTION statement followed by the name of the function. As soon as you press Enter, the screen clears, and you see the starting line followed by END FUNCTION.

6 Arguments

Arguments let you pass information to a function or procedure. When the DisplayNumber procedure evaluates the expression Number$(Num%), it first assigns I% the value stored in Num% and then starts executing at the first line of the Number$ function.

7 Returning the Value

Functions return the value that you store in the variable named by the function. Here, the function is named Number$. When "five" is stored in Number$ and the END FUNCTION statement is reached, the value returned is the string "five".

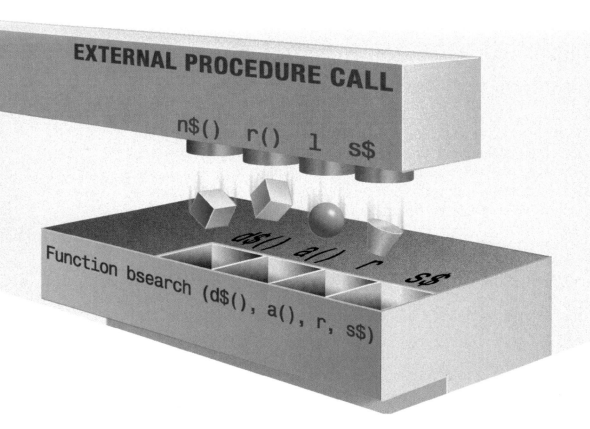

PART 2

Data Types, Constants, and Variables

As far as the computer is concerned, everything is stored as bits and bytes. The text you see on your computer screen is just an interpretation of the bytes stored in your computer's memory. When you write programs, you tell your computer how to interpret and manipulate data to produce meaningful output.

From the very start, QBasic knows how to interpret certain things, like whole and fractional numbers. The lessons in this part introduce data types, constants, and variables— the work spaces of your programs.

6 A Variable by Any Other Name

7 Giving Variables a Value

8 To Be Precise

9 Whole Numbers

10 Character Strings

11 Arrays and Tables

12 New Structures from Old

Data Types

A *variable* is a chunk of your computer's memory that has a name, like Address or Salary, and occupies several bytes of computer memory. But information, stored as bytes in memory, doesn't really mean much to the computer or to QBasic. A sequence of bytes can contain a program, data, or just garbage. For QBasic to interpret and use whatever is stored in the computer's memory, variables must have an associated *data type*.

QBasic has five data types: integers, long integers, single- and double-precision numbers, and character strings. Each of these data types, when associated with some variable, tells QBasic how to interpret what is stored in the memory belonging to the variable.

For example, long integers and single-precision numbers are always four bytes long. Suppose that Whatever is a long integer variable that contains the number 1,078,530,011. But, if the same bytes of memory were misinterpreted as a single-precision number, the interpretation of their value comes out to be 3.141593! The figure shows how data types affect the interpretation of your computer's memory.

Variables and Constants

Variables are chunks of computer memory that have an associated data type telling QBasic how to interpret the data stored in that chunk. At a more abstract level, however, you can think of variables as simply storage places that hold one particular type of data temporarily. The key feature of variables is that a variable's value can change as your program runs. In fact,

variables are nothing more than scratch areas where you store the data and intermediate calculations that your program is working on.

Special Characters That Determine Data Type

The most common way to specify the data type of a variable in QBasic is to add a special character to the end of the variable name. The special symbols that QBasic uses to indicate data types are these:

Symbol	Data Type
! (or none)	Single-precision
#	Double-precision
%	Integer
&	Long integer
$	Dynamic character string

For example, X% is an integer variable because its name ends with the special character %. The special characters are actually part of the variable name, so X$ is a dynamic character string variable because it ends in $, but it is altogether different from the X% variable.

It is easier to understand the use of variables when you contrast them with *constants*. Like variables, constants also have a data type. However, while variables are allowed to change as your program runs, constants cannot change. For example, the long integer you saw previously—1,078,530,011—is a constant. Its value will always be 1,078,530,011, and this fact cannot be changed.

Yet the fact that constants never change their value does not make them useless components of your programs. The first time you use a variable, QBasic sets its value to 0. Sometimes this is what you want, but often your program might need a variable to start at some other value. For example, suppose that you are doing an odd sales tax calculation in which everyone is taxed $2.50 plus a percentage of each item purchased. If you use a variable like `TotalTax` to hold the total tax amount, you would want `TotalTax` to start at 2.50 and not at 0. To do this, your program must tell QBasic to put 2.50 into `TotalTax` before you start computing the total tax. This is accomplished with an *assignment statement* that copies the constant 2.50 into `TotalTax`.

WHAT DOES IT MEAN?

An *assignment statement* tells QBasic to copy a value into a variable. Assignments are performed with the *assignment operator* (=) or with the LET statement. For example, to copy the value 2.50 into the variable `TotalTax`, you would give QBasic the statement LET `TotalTax` = 2.50 or just `TotalTax` = 2.50. Both these statements put the value 2.50 into the variable `TotalTax`. Assignments are covered in detail later, but they are needed from the very start.

Arrays

Arrays are special variables. In fact, *arrays* are blocks of variables having the same data type that are all accessed with the same name. Without arrays, some programs would be difficult to write and maintain. For example, if you want to write a program that asks the user for 100 names and addresses, sorts the names alphabetically, and then prints the names to a printer, you need to use 100 variables (`Name1$`, `Name2$`, ..., `Name100$`) to keep the names and 100 variables (`Address1$`, `Address2$`, ..., `Address100$`) to keep the addresses. Sorting the names would be a nightmare! With arrays, all the information

is stored in only *two* special variables `Name$` and `Address$`. You learn more about arrays and array access in Lesson 11, "Arrays and Tables."

Character Strings

Character string variables are also special variables. When a variable has any of the numeric data types like integer or double-precision, QBasic has an interpretation for the memory associated with the variable, as you have already seen. However, QBasic does not interpret what is inside character string variables. You can store whatever you want in character strings. The only price you pay is that you are responsible for understanding and manipulating what is in the character variable.

QBasic has many powerful tools for manipulating strings. For more information see Part 7, "Strings and String Manipulation."

Understanding the Concepts

The best way to learn about variables, constants, and data types is to use them. The next several lessons introduce these concepts to you. Be sure you try out the programs! You will get lots of practice with these things in later lessons, so don't be overwhelmed with details right now. After you get deeper into programming in QBasic, variables, constants, and data types will come naturally, so you will be able to concentrate on your programs.

LESSON 6
A Variable by Any Other Name

```
1  'Give some variables a few values
2  LET Pos.Max = 3.402823E+38          ◄── 3
   LET Neg.Max = -3.402823E+38

   ' Look at the contents
   PRINT Pos.Max
   PRINT Neg.Min   ◄──────────────────── 4
   PRINT X

5  ' Explicitly single-precision
   LET Foo.Lounge! = 3.141
6  DIM Foo.Bar AS SINGLE
```

The default data type for variables in QBasic is the single-precision numeric data type. Single-precision variables can hold fractional numbers like 3.001 and 1000.52 with a fair amount of precision. The example program in this lesson helps you explore what single-precision numbers provide for you when you use them in your programs.

1 Default Variable Names

By default, QBasic assumes that variables are single precision if they do not have any special character (!, #, % or $) as the last character of the name. Here, Pos.Max is a single-precision variable.

2 Setting Limits

Single-precision variables (and single-precision constants) have seven digits of accuracy and can range from 3.402823E+38 to 2.802597E-45 or -2.802597E-45 to -3.402823E+38. QBasic needs four bytes of memory to store each single-precision number.

22

3 Assignment Statements

You use an assignment statement to assign a value to a variable. You can assign any valid value to a variable, including another variable or a more complex *mathematical expression* such as 3 + 5. The next lesson, "Giving Variables a Value," covers assignments in detail.

4 Displaying a Variable

The PRINT statement lets you see the contents of a variable on-screen. These lines print the contents of some of the variables. Notice that the variable X was never assigned a value; PRINT X displays 0. QBasic does not complain if you do not give a variable some initial value; the first time you use it, it is assigned a value of 0.

5 Making the Type Explicit

Even though QBasic assumes that a variable is single-precision, your programs will be easier to understand if you explicitly indicate the data type by adding an exclamation point (!) to the end of the variable name. When you add an exclamation point (!) to the end, QBasic knows for sure that the variable holds a single-precision value.

6 Dimensioning the Type

Another way to make QBasic aware of the type of a variable is with the DIM (dimension) statement. QBasic uses the keyword SINGLE to recognize single-precision variables; so to declare, for example, that the variable Foo.Bar is single-precision, you could put the statement DIM Foo.Bar AS SINGLE. DIM is a powerful statement that you see used again in the lessons that follow.

Reserved words   Identifiers and symbols   Strings and numbers   Comments

Giving Variables a Value

```
' Assign some variables
LET Pos.Max = 3.402823E+38

' This line would be illegal
'
LET X + 3 = 5 + X / 2

' Show how QBasic copies values
PRINT Temporary
PRINT Pos.Max
Temporary = Pos.Max
PRINT Temporary
PRINT Pos.Max

' Stuff an integer into a single-precision
DIM Thing AS INTEGER
Thing = 4096
Z = Thing

' Alas, LET is not necessary
X = 3.141
```

1 **2** **3** **4** **5** **6**

The first time you use a variable in your program, QBasic sets it to zero. Of course, variables would be useless if there were no way to store some value besides zero in them.

The LET statement lets you store a value in a variable. The next example uses data types that you see in later lessons. The explanations cover these lines, but putting values into variables is the point of this lesson.

1 The LET Statement

The LET statement is used to tell QBasic that you want to store a value in a variable. The part of the statement to the right of the equal sign is called the *right-hand side* and the variable getting the value is called the *left-hand side*.

2 Assignments versus Equations

Assignment statements are not like equations. In algebra, you can have the equation $x + 3 = 5 + x / 2$, and, because the precedence of operators in algebra is the same precedence used by QBasic, you discover that x must be 4. QBasic cannot handle equations like this. The left-hand side of an assignment must be a variable, but the right-hand side can be anything that can evaluate to the type of the left-hand side. In other words, the right-hand side can be anything that can be stored in the variable (a number or character, a constant, another variable, or an expression like `X - 1.5` combining these). You already saw this in the last lesson. The next several lessons show you other things you can store in variables.

3 Storing Values

QBasic computes the right-hand side of an assignment and stores this value in the variable on the left-hand side. Whatever value was in the variable before is destroyed.

4 Copying Values

If you assign the value of one variable to another, the value in the source variable does not change. These `PRINT` statements make this point clear. The first two `PRINT` statements display 0, the initial value of `Temporary`, and 3.402823E+38, the value of `Pos.Max`. After the assignment statement, the next two `PRINT` statements display 3.402823E+38 twice. `Temporary` has been changed by the assignment, but `Pos.Max` remains the same because QBasic only copies the result or value of the right-hand side, but does not modify it!

5 Integers

An integer is basically a whole number between -32768 and 32767. Lesson 9, "Whole Numbers," covers integers in detail. The point here is that the value of an integer variable can be stored in a single-precision variable without problems because the value of the integer is within the range allowed by single-precision variables.

6 Saving Typing

After all this, the `LET` statement is not really necessary. When QBasic sees a line like `X = 3.141`, it knows that this is an assignment. `LET` makes things perfectly clear, but it is also very cumbersome. Because `LET` is understood in assignment statements, most programmers simply leave it off.

Reserved words   Identifiers and symbols   Strings and numbers   Comments

LESSON 8

To Be Precise

```
' Give some variables a few values
LET Pos.Max# = 1.79769313486231D+308
LET Neg.Max# = -1.79769313486231D+308

LET Pos.Max! = 3.402823E+38

' Look at the contents
PRINT Pos.Max#
PRINT Pos.Max!
PRINT X#

' Explicitly double-precision
DIM Foo.Bar AS DOUBLE
' This would give you an error
' Foo.Bar! = 3.141
Foo.Bar = 200
PRINT Foo.Bar
```

1 → LET Neg.Max#

2 →

3 →

4 → DIM Foo.Bar AS DOUBLE

5 → Foo.Bar = 200

Lesson 6 introduced single-precision numbers. QBasic has another way to store fractional numbers with much more precision and range: double-precision numbers.

Look over the next program carefully to see how different double- and single-precision numbers are!

1 Naming Conventions

By default, QBasic assumes that variables without special characters on the end are single-precision variables. If you want to use double-precision variables, you must tell QBasic this explicitly. One way is to put the hash symbol (#) at the end of the identifier. The other way to tell QBasic that a variable should be double-precision is to use the DIM statement. You'll see this shortly.

2 Setting Limits

Double-precision variables and constants hold values that are within 15 digits of accuracy and can range from 1.79769313486231D+308 to 4.940656458412465D-324 and -4.940656458412465D-324 to -1.79769313486231D+308. To get this accuracy and range, double-precision numbers need eight bytes of memory.

3 More on Naming Conventions

Although QBasic uses the hash symbol to identify a double-precision variable, it also uses the character as part of the variable name. This means that Pos.Max# is not the same variable as Pos.Max!. Look at the output of this program. The PRINT statements after this assignment make this difference clear. The first PRINT statement displays 1.79769313486231D+308, the value of Pos.Max#, while the second statement displays 3.402823E+38, the value of Pos.Max!. The special characters at the end of these identifiers make them two different variables in the eyes of QBasic.

4 Dimensioning the Type

You also can use DIM with double-precision numbers. QBasic uses DOUBLE to recognize double-precision numbers. The line DIM Foo.Bar AS DOUBLE tells QBasic that the variable Foo.Bar is now double-precision.

5 Naming Problems

When you use DIM to give a type to a variable, QBasic does not need the special character to know the type of the variable. The variable Foo.Bar declared on the previous line is now double-precision, even though it does not have the hash symbol! However, after you use DIM to declare the type of a variable, you cannot use the same first name with different type characters. Now, for example, the statement Foo.Bar! = 0 gives you a Duplicate Definition error.

LESSON 9
Whole Numbers

```
' Give some variables a few values
'LET Max% = 32767
LET Min% = -32768                          ← 2
LET Max& = 2147483647
LET Min& = -2147483648

' Look at the contents
PRINT Max%
PRINT Max&                                 ← 3
PRINT X%
PRINT Y&

' Explicitly integer and long integer
DIM Foo.Bar AS INTEGER
DIM Foo.Lounge AS LONG
' This would give you an error
' Foo.Lounge% = 1000
Foo.Bar = 20.50
Foo.Lounge = -1000.50
PRINT Foo.Bar
PRINT Foo.Lounge
```

1
4
5

The fractional numbers QBasic supports with single- and double-precision numbers are fine for many things like financial computing. But, there are some cases where whole numbers are all that are needed.

QBasic has two types of whole number, or integer, variables, based on their range. This lesson introduces you to integers and long integers.

1 Naming Conventions

To use integers and long integers, you need to put special characters at the end of the variable names. If you want a variable to hold an integer, you must put the % character at the end of the variable name. The & character indicates long integers.

2 Setting Limits

Integers and long integers store only whole numbers. Integers can hold any value between 32,767 and -32,768. Long integers have a much larger range, allowing values between 2,147,483,647 and -2,147,483,648. Integers occupy only two bytes of memory, while long integers need four bytes. Notice, however, that long integers always have as many as 10 digits of accuracy. Double-precision numbers need twice as many bytes to get at least this kind of precision! There is a trade-off between keeping fractions and just storing the whole part of a number.

3 Different Types Mean Different Names

Just as with the other data types you have seen so far, QBasic uses a special character to distinguish variable names. `Foo.Bar%` is an integer variable, different from `Foo.Bar&`, which is a long integer variable!

4 Using DIM

The `DIM` statement also can be used to tell QBasic that a variable is supposed to hold only integer or long integer values. QBasic uses the `INTEGER` and `LONG` keywords to distinguish these variable types.

5 What Integers Can Hold

As with all the variable types you have seen so far, QBasic lets you put any value in a variable, as long as the value is in the right range. For example, QBasic does not give an error if you try storing a number with a fraction into an integer variable.

LESSON 10

Character Strings

```
' Give a variable a value
1 ──► LET MyString$ = "This is a string"

2 ──►  ' This would give you errors
3 ──►  ' X$ = 1000
       ' V# = "50.5"

       ' Try out a fixed-length string
4 ──► DIM Some.String AS STRING * 10
      Some.String = "This string has more than ten characters"
      PRINT Some.String
      Some.String = "About ten"
      PRINT Some.String; "(notice the space at the end of ↵
          Some.String)"

       ' Explicitly a string
5 ──► DIM Foo.Bar AS STRING
      Foo.Bar = "Testing!"
```

Character strings, or strings for short, are special animals in QBasic. Strings can contain anything you want, and this makes them one of the most powerful tools that QBasic has to offer!

This lesson introduces you to string variables and constants. Part 7, "Strings and String Manipulation," discusses character strings.

1 Naming Conventions

Two types of character strings are used in QBasic. The first type is a dynamic string. Dynamic strings can change their length as your program runs. If you want a variable to hold a dynamic string, you must put the special character $, often pronounced *string*, after the name, as in MyString$. The other type of string, called a fixed-length string, is allocated one length for its lifetime. A fixed-length string does not have any special characters that set it apart from other variables. You will see how to create fixed-length string variables shortly.

30

2 Setting Limits

Dynamic strings that would be stored in a variable such as `MyString$` contain some number of characters. For example, `MyString$` is being assigned the string `"This is a string"`. After the assignment, the `MyString$` variable contains the 16 characters `"This is a string"`. QBasic lets you use string variables that contain up to 32,767 characters!

3 What Can Be Stored

Before this lesson, you experimented with numeric variables like `I%` and `V#` that hold numbers. As long as a number is in the right range, QBasic has no problem storing it in a numeric variable. Character string variables, however, can only hold character strings, like `"This is a string"`. This does not alienate string and numeric variables. In Part 7, "Strings and String Manipulation," you will see the many ways that QBasic works with character strings.

4 Fixed-Length Strings

Fixed-length string variables always hold character strings of the same length. For example, a fixed-length string variable that has room for only five characters can be assigned a character string with 1,005 characters, but only the first five are kept.

To make a variable hold a fixed-length string, QBasic needs the `DIM` statement. For example, `DIM Some.String AS STRING * 10` tells QBasic that `Some.String` is a string variable that always has 10 characters in it. Look at the output of the next `PRINT` statement to see the effects of this. The first `PRINT` line displays This string because QBasic chops off the part of the string that extends beyond the allocated length of `Some.String`. The second `PRINT` line displays About ten. Notice the space at the end of About ten? QBasic added spaces to the end of `Some.String` to make it exactly 10 characters in length!

5 Using DIM

The `DIM` statement also can be used with dynamic strings. QBasic uses the `STRING` keyword to distinguish strings from other types. Unlike fixed-length strings, dynamic strings do not have the length after the keyword.

WHAT DOES IT MEAN?

A *character string* is a variable that can contain arbitrary sequences of up to 32,767 characters. Strings hold information like names, such as "John Doe", and addresses, such as "123 Melody Drive". QBasic has two kinds of character strings: *dynamic* and *fixed-length strings*. The length, in number of characters, of dynamic strings is allowed to change as your program runs. Fixed-length strings are allocated one length for their lifetime. You can store strings that are longer or shorter than this in fixed-length strings, but QBasic adjusts the string to fit within the allocated length.

WHY WORRY?

The asterisk (*) must be used with the `DIM` statement for fixed-length strings. QBasic gives you an error if you do not include this character.

Reserved words   Identifiers and symbols   Strings and numbers   Comments

LESSON 11
Arrays and Tables

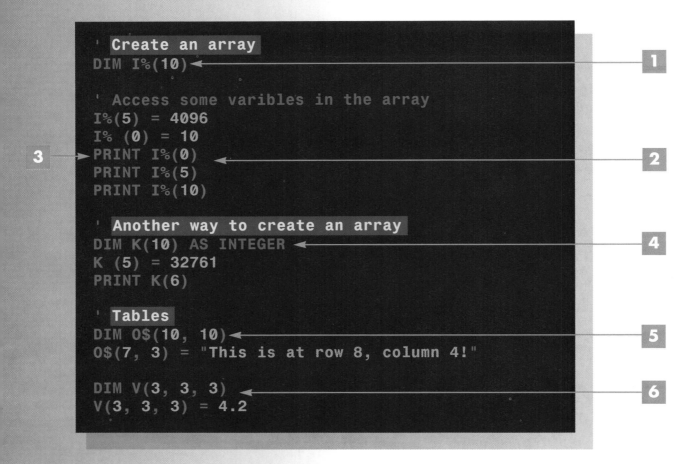

```
' Create an array
DIM I%(10)                                              1

' Access some varibles in the array
I%(5) = 4096
I% (0) = 10
PRINT I%(0)                                             2
PRINT I%(5)
PRINT I%(10)

' Another way to create an array
DIM K(10) AS INTEGER                                    4
K (5) = 32761
PRINT K(6)

' Tables
DIM O$(10, 10)                                          5
O$(7, 3) = "This is at row 8, column 4!"

DIM V(3, 3, 3)                                          6
V(3, 3, 3) = 4.2
```

3

Arrays are chunks of memory that contain several variables of the same type. All these variables are named by a single variable, like I% or V$. Arrays are an extremely powerful feature of QBasic.

1 Another Use for DIM

So far, you have seen the DIM statement used to give variables a type. DIM is not absolutely necessary for this because QBasic can figure out the type of the variable from its name, like I% or V$. But, when you use arrays, you must use the DIM statement to tell QBasic how many variables an array holds. For example, the statement DIM I% 10) tells QBasic that I% is an array of 10 integer variables.

2 Accessing Arrays

When you access an array, you get a particular variable of the array. Arrays use an *index number* to access a particular variable within an array. For example, `I%(5)` is the fifth array element (5 is the index number). `I%(5)` is an integer variable, just like `J%`, and can be used the same way you use other variables.

3 Array Index 0

Actually, `DIM I%(10)` tells QBasic to make room for *11* integer variables. The first index that QBasic enables you to use is 0. So, `I%(0)` is really the *first* variable in the array and `I%(10)` is really the *11th*. However, QBasic does not mind if you ignore the 0-index variable of an array, and doing so can make your programs easier to read!

4 Giving `DIM` a Type

The `DIM I%(10)` statement made room for 11 integer variables. QBasic knew to use integers because of the `%` character. But, you also can use a statement like `DIM K(10) AS INTEGER` just the same. `K(5)` is an integer variable in this case.

5 Tables

If your program uses tables, such as for storing account activity for several periods, QBasic has a way to do this. The `DIM` statement can be used to create tables with rows and columns of variables of one type. For example, `DIM Q$(10,10)` tells QBasic that `Q$` is an array of 121 variables: 11 rows and 11 columns. `Q$(7,3)` is the string variable in the eighth row and fourth column.

6 More than You Need

QBasic does not stop here. If you need more complicated tables, you can have as many as 60 dimensions! Three is usually more than enough, as this line shows.

LESSON 12
New Structures from Old

```
' Define a new type
TYPE MyNewType
    Age AS INTEGER
    Height AS SINGLE
    FullName AS STRING * 45
    Address AS STRING * 120
'   BadField1 AS STRING
END TYPE

' Create a variable with this type
DIM MyVar AS MyNewType

' Access some fields
MyVar.Age = 22
MyVar.Height = 5.75
MyVar.FullName = "Orlando"
MyVar.Address = "400 Forever Avenue"

' This won't work:
' PRINT MyVar
PRINT MyVar.FullName
```

1
2
3
4
5
6
7

Sometimes the variable types, called *intrinsic types*, that QBasic gives you are not enough. QBasic has an easy way to add your own types, called *structures*, to the language with the TYPE...END TYPE statement. TYPE...END TYPE tells QBasic how to interpret the new type.

MyNewType, which tells QBasic the name of the structure. The new type definition must then end with the END TYPE statement. Between these two lines, you must explain what the structure contains. The structure name cannot have any periods in it, however.

1 Starting Things Off

The TYPE...END TYPE statement has two initial requirements. First, you need a line like TYPE

2 Fields

In many ways, a structure is a packet of variables. Consider an application with blanks for `FullName`, `Address`, `Age`, and `Height`. Each of these blanks is a *field* that can contain some type of information. The `FullName` and `Address` can hold character strings, `Age` can hold an integer, and `Height` can hold a single-precision number.

3 Defining Fields

Structures let you put variables inside other variables. Between the `TYPE` and `END TYPE` statement, you can list each variable that the structure contains on a separate line. However, you must give QBasic the type of each variable, such as `Age AS INTEGER`. You should recognize this format from the `DIM` statement, except the actual `DIM` part is missing.

4 String Fields and Arrays

When you use strings inside structures, you are restricted to using fixed-length strings. Unfortunately, you cannot put arrays inside structures.

5 Using the Type

Now that you have defined the new structure, you need to create a variable to hold the information. Suppose that you have defined the type `MyNewType`. To create a variable `MyVar` to hold information for this structure, you say `DIM MyVar AS MyNewType`.

6 Accessing the Fields

Now that you have created a type and a variable, you need to access the fields of the variable. The period symbol (`.`) is used to tell QBasic which field you want access to. `MyVar.Age` is an integer variable. This variable is actually the `Age` field of `MyVar`.

7 Intrinsic Types

Although QBasic lets you create new types, it only knows how to deal with the intrinsic types: integers, long integers, single- and double-precision numbers, and strings. The statements and operators that come with QBasic, such as `PRINT`, addition (+), subtraction (-), and all the others, are designed to use only these intrinsic data types. Since structures only **hold** information, you are responsible for picking out the right parts, the fields with intrinsic data types, and using them as arguments to these statements and operators.

PART 3

Basic Input and Output

QBasic provides several ways to gather input from the user and to generate output. In this part, you learn about a few of these methods so that from the very start your programs are doing useful work.

Getting Input from the User

If you want your program to respond and adapt to the user, you need to have some way of getting data from the user into your program. Every program that does something useful requires input. Even QBasic itself needs input. The input you give QBasic is really your program. The job of QBasic is to start your program and do exactly what you have written.

QBasic lets you get all sorts of input from the user. In fact, using the INPUT statement, QBasic lets you get data from the user in any one of the five data types that it supports. There are many other ways to get input from the user, and by the end of this part, you will be able to write programs that use most of them.

Generating Output

Just as every program needs to receive data from the user, every program also must give information back to the user. Once your program has taken some input and processed it, it must let the user know the results of the processing. When your program tells the user something like this, the program is said to generate output.

13 Input from the Keyboard

14 Output to the Screen

15 Formatted Output

16 Columns Like You Want Them

17 Waiting for that Special Key

18 Getting Data Directly from Your Program

19 Looking for DATA

20 Sending Output to a Printer

Part 3: Basic Input and Output

There are many ways for your programs to generate output from QBasic, but none of them are complicated to use or to understand. The QBasic PRINT statement is one way, and, in fact, the easiest way to generate output. For example, if you want to tell the user what his or her tax is going to be, you might use a line like PRINT "Your tax is"; Tax in your program, assuming that it has somehow input the user's tax information and done all the right calculations so that the variable Tax holds the right value.

The PRINT statement is fairly versatile, but it doesn't give you much control over the format of the things it tells the user.

The line PRINT 10250.3, for example, always displays 10250.3 on-screen. But, what if this is supposed to be a dollar amount? QBasic has an easy way to let you tell it how you want output generated with a special string called a format string. You will learn more about format strings, and many other ways QBasic gives you to format your output nicely, in just a moment.

This figure shows the process of communicating with the user through input and output statements. The statements command QBasic to get input from the user or to write data to the display.

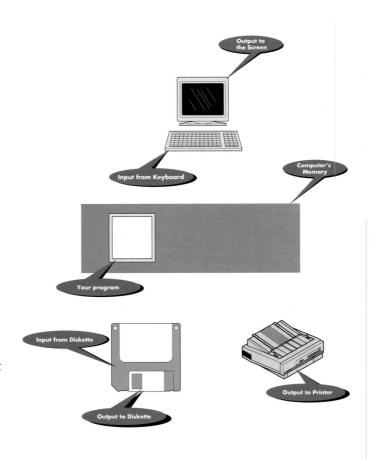

Using the input and output mechanisms of QBasic to communicate with the program's user.

Keeping Input in Your Programs

The most important kind of input is input that comes from the user. You write programs to process data and generate useful output. Sometimes, however, you need to get information into your program without bothering the user for the information.

Consider the tax program again. This tax program would not be terribly useful if it told the user, "All right, now look up your tax in the tax table at the back of your booklet." Your tax program is supposed to relieve the user of this kind of hassle! Because the tax tables only change periodically, it would be nice if you could keep the tables inside your program, and let your program access the information when it is needed.

One way to do this is with the READ and DATA statements. The READ statement is much like the INPUT statement, but it gets input from the DATA statements you scatter throughout your program rather than from the user at the keyboard. You will read more about these two statements later.

Generating Hard Copies

The output your programs generate is fine for most things. But, information you display on the screen is not permanent. If the screen is cleared or if it scrolls up because of new output, what was there is gone. You can generate printed copies, also called hard copies, of your program's output. The LPRINT statement acts exactly like the PRINT statement except that output goes to the printer rather than the screen.

Moving On from Here

Input and output are the most important parts of any program. Although this part only covers some of the basics, once you master these, you are well on your way to writing usable and useful programs!

Input from the Keyboard

```
     ' Gimme data!
1 ──▶INPUT A, B$, C
     PRINT "A = "; A
     PRINT "B$ = "; B$
     PRINT "C = "; C

     ' A little nicer...
2 ──▶INPUT "Can I have a number"; X
3 ──▶INPUT "How about a string and another number?", Y$, Z

     ' Q$ is not the prompt here, but an input variable
     Q$ = "This string gets changed by the next statement"
4 ──▶LINE INPUT Q$
     PRINT "Q$ = "; Q$

     ' Inputting strings with special characters
5 ──▶LINE INPUT "Name and address, please: "; A$
6 ──▶LINE INPUT ; "Age: "; Age$
     PRINT "...Thanks!"

     ' This prompt is asking too much
7 ──▶INPUT "I dare you to enter a string with a comma in
     it! ", B$
```

There are many ways to get input from the keyboard. There are two extremes: input mechanisms that make QBasic do most of the work, and input mechanisms that make you do most of the work.

The sample program for this lesson covers the INPUT and LINE INPUT statements. The INPUT statement is easy to use because QBasic does nearly all of the work. LINE INPUT is also easy to use, even though you are left with some work to do yourself.

1 Getting Data in

If you want to read information from the user, the INPUT statement is one way to do it. After the INPUT statement, you list the variables that you want filled in, separated with commas.

2 Prompt Strings

The INPUT statement lets you provide a *prompt string* that is displayed in place of the question mark when QBasic reads data. The prompt string allows you to inform the user of the data QBasic is requesting. If you enter INPUT "Can I have a number"; X, QBasic, by way of the semi-colon, adds a question mark to the prompt string.

3 Question Mark Not Included

To omit the question mark at the end of the prompt string, place a comma between the prompt string and the first variable being read.

4 One String at a Time

LINE INPUT allows you to specify one string variable for input. If you try the statement LINE INPUT I% in a program, QBasic will give you a Type Mismatch since I% is an integer variable instead of a string. LINE INPUT lets you enter up to 255 characters in the string variable.

5 Prompt String

LINE INPUT allows you to specify a prompt string; however, unlike INPUT, LINE INPUT never prints an extra question mark.

6 More to Come

Normally, when the user presses Enter after entering data for INPUT or LINE INPUT, QBasic moves to the next line on the screen; however, this default action might not be desired. LINE INPUT and INPUT let you specify certain actions after you press Enter. If you place a semicolon between INPUT or LINE INPUT and the prompt string, QBasic does not move to the next line when you press Enter. In this lesson, the message "...Thanks!" is displayed on the same line as the age you enter.

7 No Commas

INPUT uses commas to determine the separation of entered data. This presents a problem when a string contains commas. To overcome this problem, enclose the string with quotes as in "Banana, Orange". Without the quotes this string is taken as two separate variables with INPUT while the quotes tell INPUT to treat the string as one contiguous string.

WHY WORRY?

When QBasic executes an INPUT statement, it displays a question mark to request input from the user. If the statement is INPUT A, B$, C, QBasic expects the user to enter a number, a string, and another number separated by commas. If the information entered does not match the variables' types being requested, such as Bird, Dog, 7, QBasic tells you to Redo from start and redisplays the question mark. You must enter information at the question mark to match the variables in the INPUT statement.

WHY WORRY?

The prompt string must be a string constant. It cannot be a string variable like X$, since QBasic would consider X$ to be a variable to be read in from the user. If you must use a variable to store the prompt string, you should use the PRINT statement, discussed in the next lesson, to display the prompt.

Reserved words   Identifiers and symbols   Strings and numbers   Comments

LESSON 14

Output to the Screen

```
' Initialize some variables...
X = 1
Y = 2
G# = 1.24120542045#
P$ = "The End"

' Greetings, user
PRINT "Hello world!"
PRINT

' No spaces, please!
PRINT 1; Y; 3; G#
PRINT "Hello"; "Good-bye"; "The End"
PRINT

' I can't read that!  Where are the spaces?
PRINT X, Y, 3, G#
PRINT "Hello", "Good-bye", P$
PRINT

' On and on and on...
PRINT "All of ";
PRINT "this ";
PRINT ;;;"will be on ",
PRINT 1,
PRINT "line!"
```

1

2

3

4

5

You've seen how to get data from the outside world into your program. Now it's time to see how to get data from inside your program to the outside world with the PRINT statement.

Type in and start this program. PRINT is really simple, but it has many options of which you need to be aware.

1 Quick and Dirty

The PRINT statement can be used with no frills just by putting the things you want displayed after the statement, separating each item by either commas or semicolons.

You can tell PRINT to display any variable or constant whose type is one of QBasic's five *intrinsic*, or predefined, *data types*. Integers, long integers, single- and double-precision, and strings are the only intrinsic data types that QBasic has, so you can PRINT anything that is of one of these types. You cannot, for example, PRINT whole structure variables, although you can PRINT the values of the fields they contain as long as those are one of the intrinsic types.

2 Semicolons

Semicolons and commas do special things to the INPUT statement. These symbols also have special meaning with the PRINT statement. The semicolon tells QBasic that whatever gets printed next should come immediately after what was just printed. Start the sample program for this lesson and notice how the strings "Hello", "Good-bye", and P$ appear crunched together on the line, without any spaces. The semicolons make this happen.

Why, then, do the numbers have space between them? The reason is that QBasic treats numbers in a special way. In the output for this line of the sample, QBasic has left one space for a possible negative sign. Try changing the program so the numbers are all negative. The space that came before the numbers is now gone. QBasic also puts one space after each number it prints.

3 Commas

You also can put commas between a pair of arguments in a PRINT statement. The comma acts like the Tab key on a typewriter, and it moves over to the next available column to start printing. Unlike a typewriter, the columns are fixed. There are five columns, each one 14 characters wide.

4 Dangling Separators

When a semicolon or a comma appears at the end of a PRINT statement, QBasic remembers where it left off, and the next time output is generated, the output continues at the last point.

5 Moving on

You don't have to tell PRINT to display anything at all. The PRINT statement can appear on a line by itself, and when QBasic evaluates the statement, it moves to the next line.

Formatted Output

```
' How should I be USING this thing...
A$ = "###_-###_-####"
PRINT USING A$; 123; 456; 7890

' Number Formats
PRINT USING "### "; 1; 10; 100; 1000; 10000
PRINT USING "####,.## "; 10.345; 10.34; 10250.5

' Finances...
PRINT USING "**#####.## "; 100.005
PRINT USING "**$####.## "; 100.005
PRINT USING "$$#####.## "; 100.015

' Strings!
PRINT USING "!"; "Hello"; "inverted"; "!!!"
PRINT USING "& "; "Hello"; "inverted"; "!!!"
PRINT USING "\       \"; "Hello"; "inverted"; "!!!"
```

Although PRINT lets you display data from any one of the five intrinsic types, the way it does might not be the way you want the output to look. How do you make the number 10250.5 print out as $10,250.50 without having to write your own program to do this? This program shows you how to do just that with the PRINT USING statement.

1 Using PRINT USING

The PRINT USING statement is easy to use. You simply put a string variable or string constant called the format string after the USING keyword, then list the variables or constants you want formatted this way after the format string, separated by semicolons.

2 Formatting Numbers

The format string that PRINT USING takes has many options. This line of the sample program uses PRINT USING to format numbers. When a format string contains the hash symbol "#", this tells QBasic a number should be inserted in place of the "#" in the output. The number of hash symbols you give QBasic is important. If the number that QBasic fills in has fewer digits than there are hash symbols, QBasic right-justifies the number with spaces so that exactly as many spaces are used as there are hash symbols. If the number is too big to fit in the space, the entire number *is* displayed, but a percent sign, "%", is shown immediately before it.

3 Decimals and Commas

You also can tell QBasic to format decimal numbers such as 10250.5 with commas and exactly two decimal places. To tell QBasic to display a fraction, put a period followed by one or more hash symbols after the hash symbols for the whole number part. For example, if you use the format string "#####.##", QBasic displays your numbers as fractions with two decimal places and room for five digits on the whole number side.

4 Financial Output

The PRINT USING statement has some special formatting characters for displaying financial output. If you put "**" before a string of format characters like "#####.##", QBasic fills the whole number part of the output with "*" if there aren't enough digits in the number to fill the space you provided.

Dollar signs are important in financial output, and there are two easy ways to put them into your format strings. One way is with "**$". This does the same thing as "**", but now a dollar sign is placed immediately before the number. "$$" also puts one dollar sign immediately to the left of the number, but it does not fill the extra space with "*".

5 Formatting Strings

PRINT USING also enables you to tell QBasic how to print strings with the three formatting characters "!" (exclamation), "&" (ampersand), and "\" (backslash). The exclamation "!" tells QBasic that only the first character of the string should be displayed, and the ampersand "&" tells QBasic what the entire string should be.

The backslash character "\" acts like the hash symbol. You can put as many spaces as you want between two backslashes. QBasic counts the number of spaces, including the backslashes, and only displays that many characters from the string.

6 Don't Take Me Literally

Because the format strings use some characters to mean special things, you cannot use these special characters directly in your format strings. For example, if you want to display the hash symbol inside a format string, you can't do it by using just a hash symbol ("#"). QBasic enables you to precede any of the special formatting characters by an underscore, "_", to remove the special meaning.

> **WHY WORRY?**
>
> You also can tell QBasic you want commas inserted into the whole number side when it displays a number by putting a comma before the period. The format string "#####,.##" would format the number 10250.5 as "10,250.50" in the output.

Reserved words	Identifiers and symbols	Strings and numbers	Comments

LESSON 16

Columns Like You Want Them

```
PRINT "Lesson 16..."

PRINT SPC(3); "Three spaces from the left, right?"

PRINT "Left edge...", "some text"
PRINT "Left edge...", SPC(14); "some text"
PRINT "Left edge...", SPC(14), "some text"

K% = 6
PRINT "Hello"; TAB(3); "there"; TAB(K%);
PRINT "Mr. User!"; TAB(3); "How are";
PRINT TAB(11); "you?"
```

1

2

3

When you use commas to separate items in the PRINT statement, QBasic places the items in particular columns. However, you are not stuck with the columns as QBasic has defined them.

The sample program in this lesson uses the TAB and SPC functions to position the items that you PRINT in a more versatile way.

1 The Final Frontier

The SPC function enables you to insert an exact number of spaces into PRINT statements. For example, PRINT SPC(3); "Hello" prints out three spaces followed by the string Hello.

WHY WORRY?

SPC and TAB are not really functions that you can use anywhere in your program. They can only be used with PRINT or LPRINT. There is a function which does the same thing as SPC, though, and is really a function. If you're interested, look ahead to Part 7, "Strings and String Manipulation," and read about SPACE$.

2 Tabbing Out

When the columns that QBasic uses with the comma separator are not right for you, you can use the TAB function. Like SPC, TAB can be used with PRINT or LPRINT. However, instead of telling how many spaces to insert, TAB tells QBasic that the rest of the output must start at the column you specify. So, for example, if you want to print out numbers that start 1, 20, 25, and 40 characters from the left side of the screen, put a line like PRINT TAB(1); 1; TAB(20); 2; TAB(25); 3; TAB(40); 4 into your program.

3 No Tolerance

When QBasic comes across one of these TAB functions among the items it has to print out, it takes precautions to ensure that it can print at the column you asked for by moving to the next line if necessary.

Start the sample program for this lesson and look at the output from this line. Notice that QBasic starts to print on a new line when it cannot move to the column that is asked for.

Waiting for that Special Key

```
      PRINT "Press any key..."
1  →  SLEEP

   10    PRINT "Don't press 'q', whatever you do!"
2 →15    A$ = INKEY$
      IF A$ = "" THEN GOTO 15
      IF A$ = "q" THEN GOTO 20

      PRINT "Oh, that's good.  You pressed ";
3  → PRINT CHR$(34); A$; CHR$(34)

      GOTO 10

   20    PRINT "Well, alright.  Be that way."
      END
```

There are times when you don't want or need the user to press the Enter key to process what he or she has typed. You might just want the user to strike any key.

QBasic has two ways to wait for the user to press a single key. The SLEEP statement waits indefinitely for the user to press any key. However, SLEEP does not care exactly what key the user presses. The INKEY$ function can be used instead to find out which key, like **A, Enter** or **F1**, was pressed. The next program lets you find out more about SLEEP and INKEY$.

1 Waiting for Any Key

The SLEEP statement stops your program until the user presses any key. This statement is especially useful for pausing to help the user read what is on the screen. SLEEP can, however, be a detriment to the sanity of a user unless you let him or her know that your program is waiting for a key to be pressed!

2 Finding which Key Was Pressed

The SLEEP statement just waits for any key to be pressed, then sets your program back to work. If you want to know what key the user pressed, you have to do something different. The INKEY$ function checks to see whether the user has pressed a key. If no key has been pressed, INKEY$ returns " ", a string with nothing in it. However, if the user did press a key, INKEY$ returns a string containing the key pressed.

Run the sample program, and press 7 to wake up the program. Notice how the program immediately tells you that you pressed 7. This is important to remember! SLEEP does not throw away the key you press to wake up your program.

3 Function Keys

Run the sample program and try pressing one of the function keys. Try other combinations, like Alt-G or Home. Notice how your program is printing out a string with two characters?

When INKEY$ gets special keys or combinations of keys like F1 or Alt-G, it returns a string with exactly two characters in it. The first character has a character code of 0, and the second identifies the key combination.

You can use this feature of INKEY$ to write your own subroutines to get input from the user. For example, because INKEY$ can detect the arrow keys, your input subroutine can let the user do some fancy editing of what they are entering. It's all up to you!

> **WHAT DOES IT MEAN?**
>
> Characters in a string are stored as a sequence of bytes, and each character has a byte-long character code. The ASC function lets you see what the character code is for the first character of a string. So, if ASC(INKEY$) returns 0, the user just pressed a special key or key combination. Character codes and the ASC function are covered in detail in Part 7, "Strings and String Manipulation."

LESSON 18

Getting Data Directly from Your Program

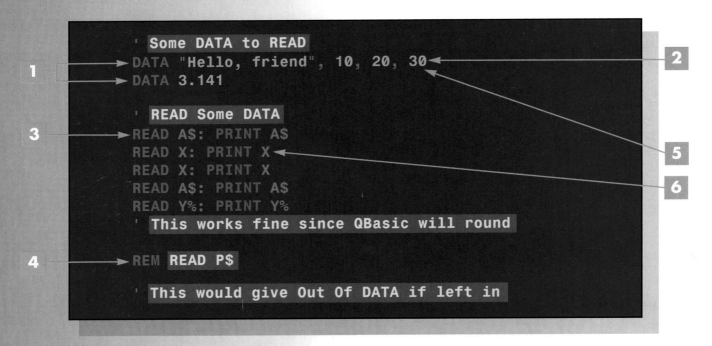

```
' Some DATA to READ
DATA "Hello, friend", 10, 20, 30
DATA 3.141

' READ Some DATA
READ A$: PRINT A$
READ X: PRINT X
READ X: PRINT X
READ A$: PRINT A$
READ Y%: PRINT Y%
' This works fine since QBasic will round

REM READ P$

' This would give Out Of DATA if left in
```

QBasic provides an easy way to store much-used data directly in your program with DATA statements. DATA statements are used with the READ statement to fill in variables with constants from the DATA statements in your program.

The program for this lesson shows you how to use READ and DATA.

1 Where to Put Your DATA

DATA statements can appear anywhere in the main module of your program. DATA statements do not do anything by themselves, so it is all right to sandwich them in any place in your programs. However, although you can put DATA statements wherever you would like, it is a good idea to keep them all in one place for readability.

2 What to Put in DATA

DATA statements can contain only one thing: constants. You can put character string constants and any type of numeric constants that you want in DATA statements. In the next step, you read about the READ statement, which lets you access the information stored in these DATA statements.

3 Getting at the DATA

The way to get at the information you put in DATA statements is with the READ statement. READ behaves much like INPUT except that information is not read from the keyboard, but from the DATA statements in your program. To use a READ statement, you just need to list the variables that you want filled with DATA, separating them with commas.

The first READ statement in your program gets the first constant in the first DATA statement. Each time QBasic fills a variable in a READ statement, it gets the information from the next constant among the DATA statements in your program.

4 Out of DATA

In most cases, READ and DATA are in what is called one-to-one correspondence. This means that each variable in a READ statement has one constant among the DATA statements. You always can put more DATA in your program than you ever will READ, but you cannot READ information that isn't there! If you try to READ into a variable, but QBasic does not have any more constants among the DATA statements, you get an Out Of DATA error.

5 Special Strings

Constants in DATA statements are very peculiar things. QBasic treats all constants that it finds in DATA statements as string constants. For example, you can have a statement like DATA Bird, Fish, 77 in your program. Bird and Fish are treated as string constants by QBasic, even though they don't have double quotes surrounding them. This also means that, although 77 is really a numeric constant, QBasic lets you READ it as a string.

6 Matching Types

You must make sure that the variables that QBasic fills with the information from DATA statements is of the right type. This means that you cannot read strings into numeric variables. Trying to do so gives you a Syntax Error.

This also means you cannot read an out-of-range value into numeric variables. For example, if you try to READ the constant 32768 into an integer variable, you get an Overflow Error because 32768 is out of range for integers.

WHY WORRY?

One of the most difficult things about using READ and DATA statements is that, if an error occurs, QBasic only marks the READ statement where the Syntax Error or Overflow occurred! You have to track down the misleading DATA statement yourself. If you always match READ statements with DATA statements, this is easy!

Looking for DATA

```
' Use RESTORE to go back to the top
DATA 1, 3, 5
READ A, B, C
RESTORE                                          [1]
READ D, E, F
PRINT A, B, C, D, E, F

' Use RESTORE with a label
RESTORE DownThere                                [2]
READ A, B, C
PRINT A, B, C
RESTORE 1000
' The next line generates an error
READ D, E, F
' There is no data past line 1000 for this READ
PRINT D, E, F


DownThere:
     DATA 100, 1000, 10000

1000     END
```

[3]

When you use READ and DATA statements in your program to initialize variables only once, you probably won't run into any problems. You have just one constant in the DATA statements for each variable you have in the READ statements, and you are done.

But, you can make the READ statement look anywhere you want to find the DATA statements. This means that you can READ the same bunch of DATA statements over and over in a program. Or, you can keep different sets of information in

your program with DATA statements, and tell QBasic to look in different places in the program for the data to READ. The RESTORE command lets you control where QBasic finds the DATA statements to be read.

Type in the next program. Read the explanations carefully before starting the program. There is an intentional error here: an Out Of DATA error.

1 RESTORE **without a Label**

When QBasic comes across the RESTORE statement in your program, the next READ statement gets its information from the first DATA statement in your program. RESTORE is useful if you are going to read the same DATA statements over and over again.

2 RESTORE **with a Label**

QBasic also lets you give the RESTORE statement a line label. A line label can be an identifier, like StartOfData, or a line number, like 10. When you give RESTORE a label, QBasic looks for the first DATA statement that it finds after that label, and the next time you use READ, the information starts at that DATA statement.

QBasic won't tell you anything if there are no READ statements on or after the label you give to RESTORE. However, if you try to READ after this, QBasic gives you an Out Of DATA error.

3 **Inside** READ **and** DATA

To better understand how RESTORE works, it helps to understand how QBasic treats READ and DATA statements internally. QBasic keeps a special marker that indicates the line, statement, and position of the next constant that READ gets. When QBasic fills in a variable from one of the READ statements in your program, it grabs the constant that this marker indicates and advances the marker to the next available DATA item.

When READ advances the marker, it positions it at the next constant in the DATA statement. But, if there are no more constants, it looks for the next DATA statement in the program. If, after all this, there are no more constants and no more DATA statements, the mark is invalidated so any more READ statements cause an Out Of DATA error.

The RESTORE statement gives you control over this marker by letting you tell QBasic to which line of DATA statements the marker should be positioned.

LESSON 20

Sending Output to a Printer

```
1 ──►  LPRINT CHR$(12); ' form feed
2 ──►  LPRINT TAB(32); "Financial Report"
       ' This gets centered
3 ──►  LPRINT STRING$(75, "-")

       ' Formatting the output using LPRINT
       LPRINT "Sales";
4 ──►  LPRINT USING "$$####.#"; TAB(20); 1000.15;↵
       TAB(40); 1000.15
       LPRINT "Marketing";
       LPRINT USING "$$####.#"; TAB(20); 10.15; TAB(40);↵
       10.15
```

Sending output to the screen is fine, but it is not permanent. If you need to make hard copies of the output your program generates, you can use the LPRINT and LPRINT USING functions to have QBasic send output to a printer attached to your computer.

Here is an example of using LPRINT and LPRINT USING.

1 Where Did it Go?

You can use the LPRINT and LPRINT USING statements as long as you have a printer attached to your computer. These two statements behave exactly like PRINT and PRINT USING except that QBasic sends the output to LPT1: rather than the screen.

2 Ejecting the Page

This line uses the CHR$ function, which you have not seen before. CHR$ gives you a character string with only one character in it, corresponding to the character code you give as argument. Here, CHR$ is used to send the form-feed character to the printer in order to advance to the top of a new page. CHR$ is covered in detail in Part 7, "Strings and String Manipulation."

3 Printing a Separator

The STRING$ function creates a character string with several repetitions of a single character in it. Here, STRING$ sends a line with 75 "-" characters to the printer. STRING$ is also covered in detail in Part 7.

4 Formatting Output to the Printer

LPRINT can do all the things that PRINT can do. The only difference is that LPRINT sends its output to the printer. If you want special control over the formatting of numbers and character strings, you can use the USING keyword to give LPRINT a format string. The syntax of LPRINT USING is no different from that of PRINT USING.

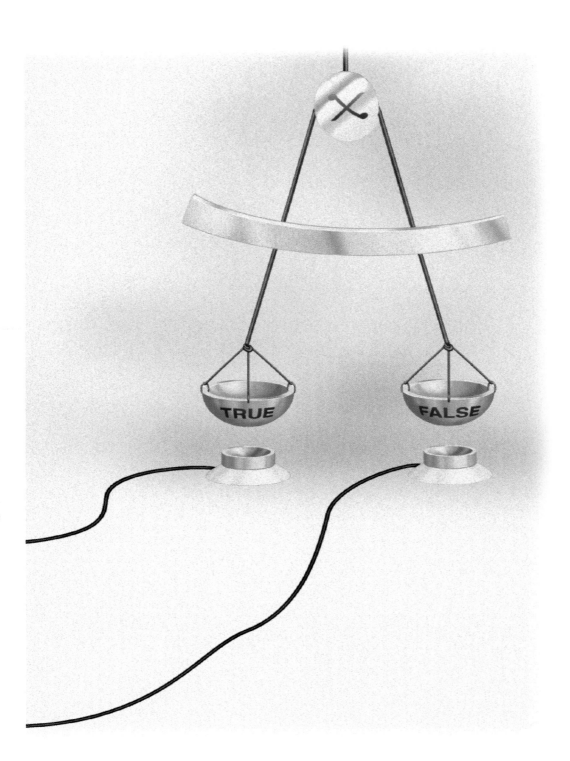

PART 4
Decisions, Repetition, and Control

Everything you do requires decisions. In the morning, you have to decide whether to hit the snooze button one more time or actually get out of bed. You have to decide what to eat, what to wear, and where to go. Your brain is even making decisions constantly without bothering to let you know! Day in and day out, regardless of the decisions you make, there are some things you do again and again. Unfortunately, intense repetitive actions tire humans quickly. But among the many things that computers do well is make fairly complex decisions quickly and perform repetitive actions without complaining or getting tired.

The lessons in this part introduce several new statements that let QBasic make decisions and repeat actions. Philosophers cannot understand how humans make decisions, but you will have no problem understanding how to give your QBasic programs a little intelligence.

Decision Making

When your programs make decisions, they do not have to bother with all the factors that humans add to their decision-making processes. There are no ethical considerations nor monetary concerns. The heart of the decision-making process with computer programs lies in comparing things. If a bank account balance becomes negative, the program takes some action related to overdrawn accounts, such as generating a statement and adding a service charge.

21 Unconditional Branching

22 Branch by Number

23 Boolean Algebra and Boolean Expressions

24 Conditional Branching

25 More Conditional Execution

26 Case by Case

27 Looping

28 WHILE...WEND and DO...LOOP

29 Jumping Out of the System

This does not mean that your programs cannot be granted some conscience so that ethical considerations and monetary concerns can be factored in. For example, you might decide to write a program to figure out a cheaper way to make road trips for salespeople. As your program plans the route for a trip from, say, Houston to Walla Walla, it decides among the various ways to travel based on cost. Your program must compare costs to find the cheaper route because it has no intuition for things like "better" or "cheaper."

But comparative decisions, or conditions, usually aren't made based on just one thing. Complicated decisions are made by joining simpler decisions into more complicated ones. If you write a program to control the thermostat on your house based on the conditions outside, you might turn down the inside temperature to 75 if it is at least 90 outside with more than 10% humidity in the house. Your program makes the decision to lower the inside temperature by making two comparisons and taking action only if both comparisons are valid.

Putting these decisions into your programs is not difficult. QBasic uses a special language called *Boolean algebra* to process decisions. Fortunately, Boolean expressions are almost exactly like their English translations. In Boolean algebra, you connect comparisons and other Boolean expressions together with the connectives AND, OR, and NOT. These connectives are called *logical operators*. For example, the Boolean expression Outside.Temp! > 90 AND Inside.Humidity! > 0.1 could be used in the thermostat controller program.

By itself, a Boolean expression does nothing. Boolean expressions are endowed with a value called the *truth value* that indicates whether the expression is True or False. If the Outside.Temp! variable has the value 91 and the Inside.Humidity! variable has the value 0.05, then the Boolean expression Outside.Temp! > 90 AND Inside.Humidity! > 0.1 is False. If the Inside.Humidity! variable increased to 0.15, the expression would be True.

But for your programs to use Boolean expressions to really make decisions, you need *flow control* statements.

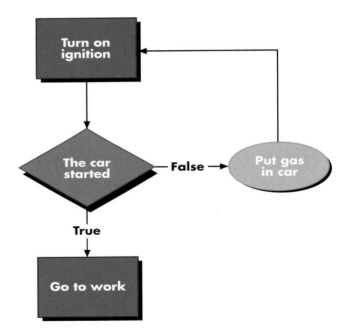

Changing Program Flow

Programs have a natural order of flow. When QBasic starts your programs, it goes to the first line in the file, executes the statement, then goes on to the next one. But programs that always go from the first to the last line are quite useless. By making decisions based on data provided to your

QBasic programs from the keyboard or other input device, your programs take alternative steps and change the natural flow from top to bottom. Repetitive actions, such as adding the interest to all the accounts in a bank, also change this natural flow because the same part of the program is executed many times.

Branching statements cause your program to change its flow, and there are several types of branches. *Unconditional branches*, also called GOTOs, change the flow of your program without having to make a decision beforehand.

QBasic has several statements that are called *conditional branching* statements. These statements are executed only if some condition is met. The IF...THEN statement is one of these conditional execution statements. For example, the thermostat controller program might have the statement IF Outside.Temp! > 90 AND Inside.Humidity! > 0.1 THEN GOTO Lower.Inside.Temp. If the temperature and humidity are indeed greater than the values 90 and .1, respectively, when QBasic sees this statement, the statement GOTO Lower.Inside.Temp will be executed. But if the temperature and humidity are less than the values 90 and .1, QBasic skips over this part and continues executing each subsequent line of code.

Loops

Besides statements that make your program take a different path based on some condition, QBasic has several statements that make parts of your program repeat. These statements are called *looping statements*, and the parts of your program that are repeated are called *loops*.

Loops are an important part of a program. You typically do not write a program to simply add two numbers and display the result. Computers are fast and designed to handle repetitive tasks. For example, at the end of the month when your bank closes your account for the month, it has a certain procedure that it follows for every account in the bank: total deposits, total withdrawals, add interest, and so on. The bank's computer processes each account by calculating the totals—thus performing a repetitive task by looping through the accounts. Computers do this sort of thing very efficiently.

There are several types of looping statements in the lessons that follow. The simplest looping statement is just a counter that executes a part of your program, setting the counter to each value in a range, such as 1 to 1,000. These loops are called FOR...NEXT loops because the loop is executed for each value in the range.

Another kind of loop, called WHILE...WEND or DO...LOOP, executes your loops based on some condition being True or False. Such loops wait until a particular condition exists, such as a variable being equal to zero, or the user entering the letter Q from the keyboard to quit a program.

WHAT DOES IT MEAN?

A *counter* is a variable used in QBasic to store incrementing values to keep track of events or loops, such as the FOR...NEXT loop. A counter, usually declared as an integer, is set to an initial value, such as 1, and incremented by any interval, such as 1,2,4,8 or even 100, to keep track of the number of times a certain action has taken place in a QBasic program.

Unconditional Branching

```
          ' Print "3...2...1...Contact!"
          GOTO Print3
   10     GOTO Print2
   20     GOTO Print1
   30     END

Print1:
              PRINT "1...";
              GOTO Contact...

Print2:
              PRINT "2...";
              GOTO 20

Print3:
              PRINT "3...";
              GOTO 10

Contact...:
              PRINT "Contact!"
              GOTO 30
```

One way to change the flow of your programs is with the GOTO statement. Normally, your programs are executed, one line at a time, from the first to the last line, stopping only to get input from the user. The GOTO statement lets you change the flow by telling QBasic to go somewhere else in your program. GOTO is called an unconditional branch because it requires no decision making by your program before it is executed. Here is a sample program with a GOTO statement.

1 Line Numbers

One way to use GOTO is by indicating the line number where QBasic continues to execute your program. You can put line numbers on blank lines to maintain continuity in your code, but numbering blank lines is not required. QBasic merely skips over blank lines until it reaches the next line of code to be executed.

2 Line Labels

The second way that QBasic allows you to change the flow of your program using GOTO is with line labels. Line labels are more descriptive than line numbers, so use line labels whenever possible.

3 Following the Flow of the Program

Computer scientists hate GOTO statements because they tend to make programs hard to follow. This program is a perfect example of how not to use GOTO. However, completely avoiding GOTO can make your programs difficult to understand too.

If you look back at the program of this lesson, the main problem with using GOTO this way is that it makes the code hard to follow. For instance, the first executable line of code states GOTO Print3. At the label Print3, the program prints 3... to the screen and branches back to line 10, which in turn branches down to Print2. You can see how this program branches all over the program and how difficult it is to follow. Now imagine a program containing 2,000 lines of code with such branching—it boggles the mind. The GOTO statement is quite useful when you need to branch to other parts of your program, but it is better to write code that is consistent—minimal unconditional branching makes code more readable and easier to maintain.

4 Printing 3...

When the program starts, QBasic sees the GOTO Print3 line and jumps down to that line of your program. QBasic continues executing your program there, and 3... gets displayed. GOTO 10 is the next line; QBasic jumps all the way back up to the line labeled 10 and continues at that line. It does not matter whether the GOTO is forward or backward in the program, as long as there is a line with that label. If no such line is found, you will get a Label Not Defined error.

5 Printing 2...1...Contact!

After 3... was printed, QBasic went back to line 10. From there, the program continues much as before and prints 2..., 1..., and then Contact!. Be sure that you follow the flow of the program yourself to see what is going on.

WHY WORRY?

You can use any nonnegative integers you want, as long as you do not repeat a line number in your program. Line numbers do not even have to be in order!

NOTE

Line numbers and line labels were discussed in Lesson 1, "Element Soup."

WHAT DOES IT MEAN?

This type of program is called *spaghetti code* because of the hard-to-follow branches. Reorder the lines so that GOTO is not needed. Be sure to leave the line labels in your modified program so that you can see how the new program differs from the lesson's program. Isn't that nicer to read?

Branch by Number

```
    ' Display the menu
Menu:
    PRINT "    Le Menu    "
    PRINT "1.   Choice #1"
    PRINT "2.   Choice #2 (quit)"

    ' Get choice
Get.Choice:
    PRINT "Your choice? "-
Get.Key:
    A$ = INKEY$
    IF A$ = "" THEN GOTO Get.Key

    ON VAL(A$) GOTO Choice1, Choice2
    PRINT "Is "; A$; " something I asked for?!"
    GOTO Get.Choice

Choice1:
    PRINT "You chose 1!"
    GOTO Menu

Choice2:
    PRINT "You chose 2!"
    ' Don't go back; choice 2 lets you leave
    END
```

1 **2** **3** **4** **5** **6**

Lesson 21 introduced the GOTO statement, which allows you to change the flow of your programs. Sometimes programs have to make decisions about data, such as printing a message when your checking account is over budget.

However, GOTO does not make any decisions about the input data; it simply directs QBasic to continue someplace else. You have to use a conditional branching statement, such as the ON...GOTO statement:

1 The Menu

Programs often have menus that direct the user through its many actions. These first few lines display a simple menu. You'll see that all it takes to print this menu is a few PRINT statements.

2 Input

The INKEY$ statement is used to get input from the user. It does not require Enter to accept what key the user presses.

3 Looking Ahead

Before diving into a description of how ON...GOTO works in this program, you need to understand the VAL function, which is covered in detail in Part 7, "Strings and String Manipulation." VAL takes a string or string variable and returns the value of the number stored in the string. For example, VAL("1") returns 1 and VAL("-10.5") returns -10.5. VAL returns 0 if the string is not a number, like "SHOE".

4 Branch by Number

ON...GOTO lets you give QBasic several possible lines to branch to and an integer that tells QBasic which line to pick. If the integer is 1, QBasic goes to the first line that you give it; if the integer is 2, QBasic goes to the second line that you give it, and so on.

5 No Place To Go

If the number that you give ON...GOTO is less than 1 or larger than the number of line labels after the GOTO, QBasic gives up and goes to the statement immediately after ON...GOTO. This is an excellent way to check for errors in input, like the menu program does here.

6 Subroutines

These groups of lines are called *subroutines*. Subroutines are segments of your program that carry out some task for the main part of the program, then continue where the main part left off. The GOTO statement returns control to the main part of the menu program. You will learn about better ways to do this later, but for now, GOTO is a good way to do this.

LESSON 23

Boolean Algebra and Boolean Expressions

```
1 ──▶ ' The truth, and nothing but the truth!
2 ──▶ 'PRINT "1 = 1 is "; 1 = 1
      'PRINT "7 < 4 is "; 7 < 4

      INPUT "Enter your salary: ", Salary!
      INPUT "...and any number: ", Num%

      ' Show the truth value of some more complex expressions
3 ──▶ PRINT "Num% > 10 OR Num% < 5 is "; Num% > 10 OR Num% < 5

      PRINT "Salary! >= 30000 AND Salary! <= 37500 is ";
      PRINT Salary! >= 30000 AND Salary! <= 37500
4 ──▶ PRINT "NOT(Num% > 10 OR Num% < 5) is ";
      NOT(Num% > 10 OR Num% < 5)

      PRINT "(Num% >= 50 AND Salary! <= 75000)
      OR Salary! > 50000 is";
5 ──▶ PRINT (Num% >= 50 AND Salary! <= 75000)
      OR Salary! > 50000
```

This lesson introduces you to Boolean algebra—the way you tell QBasic what conditions should exist before a piece of code is executed. For example, let's say that your program displays a message if the value of the variable Salary! is between $30,000 and $37,500; you would translate this condition into a Boolean expression that QBasic understands.

Boolean algebra is not difficult to learn. In fact, Boolean expressions look almost exactly like what they mean in English.

1 Relational Operators

When your program makes a decision about data, at some point it must compare (or *relate*) the data to some reference. For example, if you want your program to use a tax rate of 25% when the Salary! variable is between $30,000 and $37,500, but 35% for everything else, you are comparing Salary! to 30000 and 37500.

Lesson 23: Boolean Algebra and Boolean Expressions

2 Truth Values

The result of a comparison involving relational operators is called a *truth value*. For example, 1 = 1 is True, but 7 < 4 is False. In fact, QBasic gives True and False numeric equivalents. True is stored as -1, and False is stored as 0. So the output for 1 = 1 would be -1, and 7 < 4 would be 0.

3 AND or OR

Logical operators are special keywords that let you join comparisons into more complicated conditions. The AND operator is true only when the two expressions it connects are true. The OR operator is true if either expression is true. For example the Boolean expression Num% > 10 OR Num% < 5 will be true if the value stored in Num% is greater than 10 *or* less than 5. The expression Salary! >= 30000 AND Salary! <= 37500 is true if the Salary! variable is between $30,000 and $37,500.

4 The NOT Operator

The NOT logical operator makes true expressions false and false expressions true. NOT(Num% > 10 OR Num% < 5) is true if the value stored in Num% is *not* greater than 10 *nor* less than 5.

5 Building Complex Conditions

The power of AND, OR, and NOT comes from the fact that you can connect whole Boolean expressions with them, as in this example. This expression translates into English as "Num% is at least 50 and Salary! is not more than $75,000, or Salary! is greater than $50,000."

The AND operator returns a True value if the results of relational comparisons on both sides of the operator are True. Assume that Num% is 60 and that Salary! is $40,000. From the code, the result of the expression is True. The reason is that Num% is greater than 50 AND Salary! is less than $75,000—the conditions on both sides of the AND operator are True, so the entire expression is True.

The OR operator returns a True if the results of the relational comparisons on either side of the operator are True. You already know that the AND expression is True. The OR operator takes the result of the AND expression, and since it is True, the OR expression is True regardless of the result of the comparison Salary! > 50000.

The NOT operator reverses the result of a Boolean expression. For instance, if the result of an expression is True, the NOT operator turns it into False. Likewise, if the result of an expression is False, the NOT operator turns it into True.

> **Relational Operators**
>
> Relational operators are used to compare values to determine whether a condition exists between those variables. Relational operators perform the following comparisons: equal (=), not equal (<>), less than or equal (<=), greater than or equal (>=), less than (<), and greater than (>).

Reserved words   Identifiers and symbols   Strings and numbers   Comments

LESSON 24
Conditional Branching

```
        '  Get Salary
Get.Salary:
1       INPUT "What is your annual salary"; Salary!
        IF NOT(Salary! < 0) THEN GOTO Calculate.Tax
2       PRINT "Please enter a nonnegative salary..."
        GOTO Get.Salary

        '  Calculate taxes and decide on refund
Calculate.Tax:
3       Std.Deduction! = 2500
        Taxable.Salary! = Salary! * .1

4       IF Taxable.Salary! < Std.Deduction! THEN
            PRINT "You are entitled to a tax refund of ";
            PRINT USING "**$##,.##."; Std.Deduction! -
            Taxable.Salary!
            '  Skip next bunch of lines
            GOTO Finis
        END IF

5       IF Taxable.Salary! = Std.Deduction!
        THEN GOTO Finis

        PRINT "You owe us money!  Pay ";
        PRINT USING "**$####,.##"; Taxable.Salary! -
        Std.Deduction!
        PRINT " immediately!"

Finis:
        PRINT "Have a nice day!"
```

66

Boolean expressions are used to make decisions on data. This example uses the `IF...THEN` statement to evaluate statements *when and only when* a certain condition is True. There are two forms of the `IF...THEN` statement, so look over the program carefully.

1 Checking Input

The sample program asks you to enter an annual salary using the `INPUT` statement. The value you enter is stored in the `Salary!` variable. If you enter a value that is not less than zero, `NOT(Salary! < 0)` is True, and the statement after `THEN` is evaluated. This causes QBasic to branch to the label `Calculate.Tax`.

2 When the Condition Is False

When the condition of the `IF...THEN` statement is False, QBasic skips the line completely. Execution of your program is said to *fall through* the conditional statement.

3 Calculating Tax

This line computes the tax on the salary. The next part of the program will decide whether to give a refund or demand payment of taxes.

4 Block IF...THEN

If your program needs to do several things when a certain condition is True, you should use the block `IF...THEN` statement. This statement is like `IF...THEN` except that no statement appears on the same line as the `IF...THEN` statement. You place all the lines of code that are to be executed when the condition is true between the `IF...THEN` line and an `END IF` line. Just like the `IF...THEN` that you saw earlier, if the condition is false, QBasic picks up execution of your program after the `END IF` line.

5 Why the Condition Is False

If the taxable salary is less than the standard deduction, then the condition in the first block `IF...THEN` is true. The `GOTO` statement at the end of the block skips to the Finis line. This `GOTO` also causes execution to skip past the lines of code that tell you that you owe taxes. Notice that these lines of code are executed only when the condition is False.

WHY WORRY?

Always be sure that every block `IF...THEN` statement has an ending `END IF` statement. QBasic will give you a `Block IF without END IF` error if you try running a program without ending all your block `IF...THEN` statements.

Reserved words   Identifiers and symbols   Strings and numbers   Comments

More Conditional Execution

```
'Get an arbitrary number
INPUT "A number please: ", Number
IF Number < 0 THEN PRINT "Part I:
You entered a negative number."
PRINT "Part I: You entered a positive number."

PRINT "Part II: You entered a ";
IF Number < 0 THEN PRINT "negative";
ELSE PRINT "positive";
PRINT " number."

'Get age and tell what you can do
INPUT "Enter your age: ", Age%
IF Age% >= 21 THEN
    PRINT "You can drink, vote and drive."
ELSEIF Age% >= 18 THEN
    PRINT "You can vote and drive."
ELSEIF Age% >= 16 THEN
    PRINT "You can drive a car."
ELSE
    PRINT "You're still a bit young.  Stay home."
END IF
```

The IF...THEN...ELSE statement can be used to execute more than one statement when a condition is False. This sample program demonstrates the various ways to use the IF...THEN...ELSE statement. The first few lines contain an intentional error, so read on to see what is wrong.

1 An Error

The program first asks you to enter a number. It is supposed to tell you whether you entered a positive or negative number. Try the program out. If you enter a negative number, you get strange output in the first part. The problem is that, unless the statement after the THEN is a GOTO, QBasic continues at the next line after the IF...THEN statement, regardless of whether the condition is True or False.

68

2 Fixing the Bug

This line uses IF...THEN...ELSE to correct the error. Just like with IF...THEN, QBasic continues at the line following the IF...THEN...ELSE. However, if the condition is True, only the statement after THEN is executed, and if the condition is False, only the statement after the ELSE is executed.

3 Blocking IF...THEN...ELSE

The IF...THEN...ELSE statement can be used to execute several statements when a condition is either True or False. As shown here, the block IF...THEN...ELSE looks like the block IF...THEN statement except that a line with ELSE by itself is placed before the statements to be executed when the condition is False.

Notice that there are several entries containing ELSE IF and one containing ELSE. Each IF...THEN...ELSE block begins at the IF and ends at the ELSE. Read on to understand the difference between a line containing ELSE IF and a line containing a single ELSE.

4 Testing Several Conditions

Sometimes you need to check another condition before the ELSE statement is executed. This can be done with the ELSEIF keyword. ELSEIF must be followed by a condition. The lines following ELSEIF only execute if this additional condition is true. You can put several ELSEIF statements in a block IF...THEN...ELSE, but only one ELSE part is allowed at the end of the block.

WHY WORRY?

QBasic distinguishes ELSEIF from ELSE IF. When you use ELSE IF in a block IF...THEN...ELSE statement, QBasic still executes all the statements after the ELSE keyword if the condition is False. When you use ELSEIF, QBasic only executes the statements after the ELSEIF keyword if the new condition is True.

LESSON 26
Case by Case

```
' Get a number and make some tests
INPUT "Enter a number from 1 to 100: ", Number%

SELECT CASE Number%
CASE 1
    PRINT "Number 1!!!"
CASE 2, 3, 4, 5
    PRINT "2, 3, 4 or 5."
CASE 6 TO 10
    PRINT "Between 6 and 10."
CASE IS > 100
    PRINT "That number is larger than what I
    expected."
CASE 90 TO 99, IS < 50
    PRINT "Either between 90 and 99 or between
    11 and 50."
CASE IS < 1
    PRINT "That number is smaller than what I
    expected."
CASE ELSE
    PRINT "Thanks anyway!"
END SELECT
```

When you want to execute one of several blocks of statements based on a condition, use the SELECT CASE...END SELECT statement.

1 SELECT CASE...END SELECT

The SELECT CASE...END SELECT statement begins with a line like SELECT CASE Age% and ends with END SELECT. The first line tells QBasic which variable you are going to be testing. Any variable works, for example, SELECT CASE Name$.

2 Testing for Equality

Between the SELECT CASE and END SELECT statements you give QBasic tests to make on the variable. The lines of code that follow the test are executed only if the test is true. For example, if you want to execute several lines of code only if the variable is equal to a particular value, put the value after the CASE keyword. If the variable is equal to that value, the lines of code after the CASE keyword are executed.

3 Testing More than One Value

You can list several constants or variables after the CASE statement. If the test variable is equal to any of these values, the statements following the CASE are executed.

4 Testing a Range

You can execute a block of code *when and only when* the test variable is between two variables by giving a CASE range. For example, the statement CASE 7.5 TO 9.9 lets QBasic execute the code that follows only if the test variable is between 7.5 and 9.9.

5 Testing a Condition

You can also check to see if the variable has a certain relationship to another constant or variable. Suppose that you want to execute a block of code only if a string variable comes before the word "definition" in alphabetical order. Then you can use the CASE statement CASE IS < "definition" to make this test.

6 Combining Conditions

You can mix all these types of tests in one CASE statement. For example CASE 1, IS >= 5, 0.2 TO 0.52 lets QBasic execute the block of code that follows only if the test variable is 1, greater than or equal to 5, or between 0.2 and 0.52.

7 When All Else Fails

If none of the tests on the variable passes, you can give QBasic a block of code to execute instead. The lines of code following CASE ELSE are executed when none of the other tests pass.

> **NOTE**
>
> QBasic sees all alphabetic characters as their numerical equivalents when performing string operations. For instance, the letter A, as seen by QBasic, has a numerical equivalent of 65, while B is 66. When performing a comparison between the strings "APPLE" and "BANANA", QBasic will see the numeric representations of the characters to determine the alphabetic order of strings.

Reserved words   Identifiers and symbols   Strings and numbers   Comments

Looping

```
' Count up
Sum = 0
FOR I% = 1 TO 10                          ◄━━━━━━  1
     Sum = Sum + I%
     PRINT I%; ",";
     IF Sum > 21 THEN EXIT FOR     ◄━━━━━━  2
NEXT
PRINT

' Count down
FOR I% = 10 TO 1 STEP -4          ◄━━━━━━  3
     PRINT I%; ",";
NEXT
PRINT

' A nested loop
FOR I% = 1 TO 5
     FOR J% = 1 TO I%
  4        ━━━━━━►  PRINT J%; ",";
     NEXT
     PRINT
NEXT
```

Computers are great at doing repetitive things without complaining. This lesson shows you how to use the FOR...NEXT loop to repeat parts of your program.

1 The Counter

The FOR...NEXT loop takes a numeric counter variable (I%, in this case), a starting value (1) and a stopping value (10). When QBasic executes the FOR statement, it sets the counter variable to the starting value and then executes the lines between the FOR and the corresponding NEXT statement, called the *loop*.

When the NEXT statement of the loop is reached, QBasic increments the counter variable by one and checks to see that it has not exceeded the stopping value. If the counter has reached the stopping value, QBasic exits the loop and continues execution of the program with the line following the NEXT statement.

If the counter has not reached the stopping value, QBasic continues executing the loop until the counter reaches the stopping value.

2 Jumping Out of the Loop

Sometimes you need to leave a loop before the counter has reached the stopping value. For example, if you want to leave the loop when the Sum variable exceeds 5000, you would put the line IF Sum > 5000 THEN EXIT NEXT in the loop. This statement causes QBasic to branch to the statement following the NEXT statement and continue execution of your program from that point forward.

3 Changing the Step

If you don't want QBasic to increment the counter by 1 every time, you can change the amount, called the *step size*, by adding the STEP keyword to the end of the FOR statement. FOR I% = 10 TO 1 STEP -1 executes the loop by counting down from 10 to 1. See what happens if you change this loop so that the starting value is 1 and the stopping value is 10. How about making the starting and stopping values the same?

4 Nesting Loops

The NEXT statement of a loop is always associated with a preceding FOR statement. As shown here, the association of FOR and NEXT allows you to put loops within loops. This arrangement is called a nested loop.

In this sample, the inside loop executes completely each time the outside loop executes once. For each loop of the outside loop, its counter, I%, is incremented by 1. The counter, I%, is then used as a stopping value for the inside loop. The result of this nested loop configuration is that each execution of the outside loop provides a stopping value for the inside loop that is one higher than its previous execution.

Run this program and look at the output carefully!

Reserved words   Identifiers and symbols   Strings and numbers   Comments

LESSON 28

WHILE...WEND and DO...LOOP

```
' Print numbers less than 10
Num% = 1
WHILE Num% < 10
     PRINT Num%; ",";
     Num% = Num% + 1
WEND
PRINT

' Other ways to do this
Num% = 1
DO WHILE Num% < 10
     PRINT Num%; ",";
     Num% = Num% + 1
LOOP

DO
     A$ = INKEY$
LOOP UNTIL A$ = "Y" OR A$ = "N"
PRINT "You pressed "; A$; "!"

Sum% = 0
DO
     INPUT "Enter a number: ", Num%
     Sum% = Sum% + Num%
     IF Sum% > 10 THEN EXIT DO
LOOP UNTIL Num% = 0
PRINT "The sum is "; Sum%
```

1

2

3

4

5

QBasic has several easy ways of allowing you to execute a block of code until a certain condition becomes True or False. WHILE...WEND executes a block of code as long as some condition is True. DO...LOOP also lets you loop based on a condition. DO...LOOP can behave like WHILE...WEND, but it has many more options.

1 While a Condition Is True

The WHILE...WEND statement looks like the block IF...THEN statement. The first line begins with WHILE followed by a condition. The block of code between the WHILE and WEND is executed again and again as long as the condition is True each time the block is executed.

2 Another Way

The DO...LOOP is a much more versatile looping statement than WHILE...WEND. In fact, the DO...LOOP can do exactly the same thing as WHILE...WEND. If you want to execute a block of code again and again as long as some condition is True, you simply put DO WHILE followed by the condition at the beginning of the block and LOOP at the end of the block.

3 While a Condition Is False

An alternative to DO WHILE is DO UNTIL. However, instead of executing the loop as long as the condition is True, DO UNTIL executes the loop as long as the condition is False. After the condition becomes True, QBasic falls through the loop and continues executing your program after the LOOP statement.

4 Executing the Loop Once

If you have to execute the loop at least once before the condition is checked you can put the WHILE or UNTIL conditions after the LOOP statement, as shown here. This way the block of code is always executed at least once before the condition is checked. The example here loops until the user presses Y or N. See what happens when you move the condition UNTIL A$ = "Y" OR A$ = "N" after the DO statement and start the program.

5 Jumping Out of the Loop

Sometimes you might need to leave the loop before the appropriate condition is met. Here, for example, the program asks you to enter values in a loop, stopping when you enter 0. However, if the sum of the values you enter exceeds 10, the program leaves the loop with EXIT DO.

Jumping Out of the System

```
       ' Display Menu
Menu:
       PRINT "Make a choice:"
       PRINT "  1. STOP"
       PRINT "  2. END"
       PRINT "  3. SYSTEM"
       DO
           A$ = INKEY$
       LOOP UNTIL A$ = "1" OR A$ = "2" OR A$ = "3"

       ' Take the appropriate action
       SELECT CASE A$
       CASE "1"
           PRINT "Press F5 when you get back to the editor"
           STOP
           PRINT "Thanks!  Welcome back..."
           GOTO Menu
       CASE "2"
           PRINT "Bye!"
           END
           GOTO Menu
       CASE "3"
           PRINT "Going back to DOS...  Bye!"
           SYSTEM
           GOTO Menu
       END SELECT
```

This lesson introduces three statements for bringing your program to a halt—END, STOP, and SYSTEM.

1 The Menu

These lines of the program display a menu and wait for you to make a choice (1, 2 or 3). The program uses the INKEY$ function to get input from the user and store that input into the string variable A$. Unlike the other ways of getting input, INKEY$ does not need to wait for the user to press Enter to go on. Once you press a key, INKEY$ immediately stores the value into A$ and continues execution of your program.

2 What To Do

Processing the menu choice is handled by the SELECT CASE...END SELECT statement you saw earlier in Lesson 26. The program uses the value stored in A$ to determine which of the statements of the SELECT CASE...END SELECT statement to execute.

3 Breaking Your Program

In the early days of BASIC programming, the STOP statement was an extremely useful tool for debugging programs. When QBasic sees a STOP statement in your program, it jumps back to the editor and highlights the line of your program with the STOP statement in it. The highlight tells you that QBasic remembers where it is in your program, and if you select the **R**un menu and choose **C**ontinue (or simply press F5), QBasic will continue running your program with the statement *after* the STOP statement! To see this, start the sample program for this lesson and choose menu option **1**.

4 Ending Your Program

The END statement brings your program to a close. When QBasic evaluates an END statement in your program, it basically forgets that it was even running your program. So, unlike the STOP statement, END does not let you pick up where your program left off. In fact, if you try to continue the program, QBasic starts again from the beginning.

5 Unreachable Code

These lines of your program are called *unreachable code* because QBasic never processes them. Unreachable code does not affect the way that your programs work, but it does make them more difficult to read. If you can determine if some lines of your program are unreachable, remove them to make your program clearer to human readers.

6 Leaving QBasic

The SYSTEM statement is the harshest of the statements that stop your program. If you start your program from inside the QBasic editor, SYSTEM behaves exactly like END.

However, if you start your program from DOS, SYSTEM ends your program and exits QBasic as well.

Reserved words   Identifiers and symbols   Strings and numbers   Comments

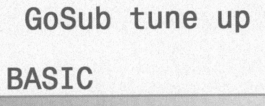

GoSub tune up

BASIC

tune up:

> NESTED
> INSTRUCTIONS

Return

PART 5

Subroutines, Procedures, and Functions

As you begin to write programs, you will find that you are frequently performing similar tasks within the programs. If you write an accounting program, for example, you might find that user data entry for checks and deposits are very similar. If you had to write the data entry portion of your program in every place within the program that required data entry, you would be repeatedly entering code fragments that were similar, if not identical. Every time you duplicate code, you could introduce small errors that would be hard to find. If you decided to change the way the data entry code operated, you would have to locate and edit every fragment of the duplicated code to properly propagate the changes.

Subroutines and functions provide a structured way to manage the parts of your programs you use frequently. The ideas in these lessons build on the idea of changing program flow, which you learned in Part 4.

30 Subroutines that Come Back

31 Branch by Number

32 Subroutines

33 Functions

34 Longer Functions

35 Subroutines that Give Something Back

The Main Routine

When QBasic starts your program, it goes to the first line in the program and starts executing the program. The program has a natural flow from the first to the last line, interrupted only by unconditional and conditional branches, and looping statements. Regardless of changes in program flow, the program has a *main routine* that consists of the lines of the program from the first to the last line. The idea of a main routine does not make much sense until it has been contrasted with subroutines.

WHAT DOES IT MEAN?

A *main routine* is the primary portion of a program from which all subroutines and functions are called. Imagine a river with many tributaries; the river is the main routine of your program, and the tributaries are the subroutines and functions.

Subroutines

Frequently, there are sections of your program that are needed by several parts of the main routine. In the accounting program discussed previously, you need to get roughly the same information for both credits and debits. Both the credit and debit parts of the program can use the same routine to get the information they need.

When part of a program is available for use by several parts of the same program, it is called a *subroutine*. Subroutines get *called* by a *calling routine* to perform some action. The credit and debit parts of the accounting program call the input subroutine to get their data.

Enabling subroutines is an important part of QBasic. Subroutines reduce errors, improve program maintenance, and make your programs more readable.

Calling and Returning

In Lesson 22 of Part 4, you typed a menu program that used ON...GOTO to switch to the action for the menu item, and then used GOTO to return to the menu display. This is fine, but what happens if you want to use the menu action someplace else in the program? The GOTO at the end of the action jumps back to the menu. This might be what you wanted, but more than likely, you wanted to perform the action, then continue doing something else before going back to the menu.

When a subroutine is called from someplace in a program, QBasic remembers where the call was made. This feature enables the call to be *returned*. So, when subroutines finish, QBasic returns to the statement after the subroutine call and continues. This means subroutines can be called from *anywhere* in your program, including from the subroutine itself! Subroutines that call themselves are called *recursive subroutines*.

This figure shows the idea of calling and returning from a subroutine with GOSUB. The arrows indicate the program flow as QBasic executes the program.

Functions

When you write subroutines, you add to the power of QBasic by defining new procedures on top of old ones. But, subroutines cannot be used inside of expressions because they do not have a value. In a tax calculation program, you might want a subroutine to compute the tax for some amount of money. You could just multiply the quantity by the tax rate, but it would be more readable to have some way to say `ComputeTax(5000,0.1)`.

Functions are special subroutines that have a value. Like subroutines, functions are called and carry out some calculation. But, when functions return to their caller, they give back the result of the calculation.

Structured Programming

Structured programming is a programming philosophy. When you write structured programs, you break your programs up into subroutines and functions that have recognizable purposes. Writing these subroutines and functions is like collecting ingredients for a recipe. Once you have all the ingredients, it is really just a matter of putting them together in the right order.

Structured programming looks at programs and programming from the bottom up. This means when you attack a problem, you decide what makes up the problem, build the parts, then assemble them into the main program. The opposite view of programming attacks the program from the top, basically ignoring the trees for the forest. The truth is, these are extremes. As you program, you need to take both approaches simultaneously.

Programming is an art, and how you program is your choice. But, structured programming makes your programs easier to understand and maintain.

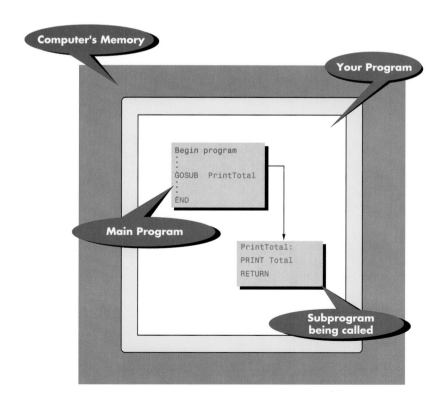

LESSON 30
Subroutines that Come Back

```
' Get the label information
INPUT "Name: ", Label.Name$
INPUT "Address: ", Label.Address$
INPUT "City, State, Zip: ", Label.City$,↵
Label.State$, Label.ZipCode$

' Jump over and print the label
GOSUB PrintLabel
GOSUB PrintLabel
GOSUB PrintLabel

' Done!
END

PrintLabel:
    PRINT Label.Name$
    PRINT Label.Address$
    PRINT Label.City$; ", "; Label.State$; "  ";↵
    Label.ZipCode$
    RETURN
```

1 ⟶

2 ⟶

3 ⟶

4 ⟶

5

When you use GOTO to change the flow of your programs, QBasic forgets about the GOTO statement and picks up execution at the new location. But, sometimes you need a way to restore the flow of the program to where it was before the GOTO. You can do this with the GOSUB statement. This program uses GOSUB to print a mailing label three times.

1 Inputting the Label

In this lesson, you are entering names and addresses to print to mailing labels in a printer. The labels that the program prints have a name, address, city, state, and ZIP code, entered by the user and stored in the variables Label.Name$, Label.Address$, Label.City$, Label.State$, and Label.ZipCode$.

2 Branching Temporarily

As you can see, the GOSUB statement looks a lot like the GOTO statement; however, when QBasic goes to the line you specify, it remembers the *caller*, or the line where the program flow changed. By remembering where the program flow changed, the program can branch out to another section of code, marked by the label PrintLabel, and then return the line following the GOSUB statement to continue program execution.

3 Printing the Label

The PRINT statement is used to display the information stored in the mailing label on your screen. Now here is an interesting little twist— if you want to print the labels to a printer, simply change PRINT to LPRINT in the statement.

4 Restoring Program Flow

Because GOSUB makes QBasic remember where the branch originated, there must be a way to restore the program to the previous statement. RETURN tells QBasic to return to the calling GOSUB statement.

5 Explicit END

When you use GOSUB and RETURN, you should be careful your program does not accidentally fall through to part of the program that has a RETURN. If QBasic tries to RETURN when no GOSUB has changed the program flow, you get a RETURN without GOSUB error. To see this, try removing this line, and rerun the program.

Reserved words   Identifiers and symbols   Strings and numbers   Comments

Branch by Number

```
' Display the menu
PRINT "  Le Menu!   "
PRINT "1. Choice #1"
PRINT "2. Choice #2"
PRINT "3. Choice #3 (quit)"

1    INPUT Choice%

2    ON Choice% GOSUB Choice1, Choice2
     PRINT "Bye!"
     END                                    5

Choice1:
3        PRINT "Action #1"
         RETURN                             4

Choice2:
         PRINT "Action #2"
         RETURN
```

The ON...GOTO statement lets you branch to a specific location in your program based on the value of a variable. QBasic also has the ON...GOSUB statement that lets you branch to a specific location, but program flow can return to the statement after ON...GOSUB through a RETURN statement.

The next program uses ON...GOSUB for a simple menu program.

1 Getting the Menu Choice

INPUT accepts an integer from the user as a menu choice. If the user enters an invalid choice, the program just ends. Try modifying the program so it tells the user the choice is invalid and asks again.

2 Making the Choice

ON...GOSUB is used to change the program flow temporarily to the appropriate menu action. Because ON...GOSUB is being used, RETURN can be used to jump back to the statement after the ON...GOSUB that changed the flow.

3 Actions

Each menu choice has an associated action. The action is carried out whenever QBasic changes program flow to the first line of the right subroutine.

4 Getting Back

In Part 4, GOTO was used to get back to the menu routine. With ON...GOSUB, RETURN brings you back to the menu routine. This is an important advantage! Because RETURN restores control to the GOSUB statement that last changed the program flow, the menu actions can be used anywhere in the program—not just from the menu routine! If you used GOTO, you would need to rewrite the routine each time you used it so that it returned to the correct line number or line label via a GOTO statement.

5 Explicit END

When everything is finished, you must end your program explicitly so it does not fall through into a subroutine that has a RETURN.

LESSON 32

Subroutines

```
' The main routine
CALL Menu.Display
INPUT Choice%
CALL Menu.Action(Choice%)

SUB Menu.Display
    PRINT "  Le Menu!  "
    PRINT "1. Choice #1"
    PRINT "2. Choice #2"
    PRINT "3. Choice #3 (quit)"
END SUB

SUB Menu.Action(I%)
    SELECT CASE I%
    CASE 1
        PRINT "Action #1"
    CASE 2
        PRINT "Action #2"
    CASE ELSE
        PRINT "What?"
    END SELECT
END SUB
```

1 **2** **3** **4** **5** **6**

GOSUB is actually an older way to handle subroutines. QBasic has a much simpler way to handle subroutines that gives you more flexibility. This program shows you how to use SUB...END SUB to write subroutines. Read over this lesson completely before typing the program.

1 The Main Routine

The main routine is where QBasic begins execution when you start your program.

2 Starting a Subroutine

To start a subroutine, type in the SUB statement followed by the subroutine name and any arguments. As soon as you press the Enter key, QBasic clears the screen and puts the cursors between the SUB statement you just entered and an END SUB. Your main routine is not gone; press F2. Every subroutine you create with SUB...END SUB appears in this listing. To return to the main routine, highlight the unindented name, and press Enter.

3 Arguments

Arguments are special variables that let you pass information to a subroutine. When QBasic starts a SUB...END SUB subroutine, it treats the subroutine like an entirely separate program. If you used the variable I% in your main routine, then called a subroutine that also used I%, the subroutine's variable would be a separate variable that exists only while QBasic is executing the subroutine. When you pass arguments to a subroutine, QBasic fills these variables with information from the calling routine.

As you can see in the lesson example, the main routine calls the subroutine Menu_Action(I%). The variable being passed to Menu_Action is the variable I%, used in the main routine to store input from the user. The value from I% in the main routine is used to fill in the parameter variable I% of Menu_Action. This variable is then used within the subroutine to execute a statement based on the value stored in I%—the original value entered by the user.

4 Ending a Subroutine

You don't need RETURN with SUB...END SUB subroutines. As soon as QBasic executes the END SUB statement, it returns to the statement that switched to the subroutine.

5 Calling a Subroutine

The CALL statement is used with SUB...END SUB subroutines to change program flow to that routine. When QBasic sees the CALL statement, it fills in the argument variables with the values you give in the CALL. Then QBasic starts executing the subroutine at the first line after the SUB statement.

6 No Explicit End

When you use SUB...END SUB, you no longer need to end your program explicitly. The subroutines you write this way are only evaluated when you use the CALL statement, so your main routine can fall through the last line without starting one of these subroutines inadvertently.

Reserved words   Identifiers and symbols   Strings and numbers   Comments

Functions

```
' Define a function
DEF FNFoo(X) = X + 1

X = 3
PRINT FNFoo(X)
X = FNFoo(FNFoo(X))
PRINT X
```

1 **2** **3** **4**

Subroutines let you extend QBasic by adding new actions to the language. Functions let you add expressions that add new mathematical or string operations to the language. Look over this program carefully. It uses the DEF FN statement to define a function.

1 Defining a Function

DEF FN associates an expression, called a *macro expression*, with an identifier. DEF FN is usually used for defining new mathematical expressions used frequently in your program.

WHAT DOES IT MEAN?

A macro expression contains an expression that is treated as part of the caller. For comparison, a subroutine contains statements and expressions, is executed as an independant block of code, and returns nothing to the caller. A macro expression is an expression executed as part of the caller and returns a result to the caller.

2 Arguments

Functions that don't take arguments are quite useless. Functions are designed to compute the result of a frequently used expression. To declare the arguments, you list the argument variables after the function name, enclosed in parentheses, and separated by commas.

3 Using an FN Function

The name of functions defined with DEF FN actually includes FN at the beginning of the function name. This means if you define a function Foo with DEF FN, the function name is actually FNFoo. You can have QBasic evaluate the function by giving the function name and all the right types of arguments.

4 What an FN Function Does

When you tell QBasic to evaluate an FN function, it plugs the values of all the arguments into the expression, evaluates the expression, and gives back the result. This means you cannot evaluate one of these functions on a line by itself. You can store the result in another variable or print the result. But, FN functions are *not* statements.

WHY WORRY?

Function Definitions

FN functions cannot contain statements. You cannot, for example, define FNPrint to be equal to PRINT X$200.

Longer Functions

```
1 →            ' Define a function
          → DEF FNDivide(Num, Den)
2 →              IF Den = 0 THEN
                     PRINT "This results in an infinite
                     value!"
                     INPUT "Enter a value to use for
                     the result: ", Result
3 →              FNDivide = Result
4 →              EXIT DEF
              END IF
              FNDivide = Num / Den
5 →    END DEF

              INPUT "Enter numerator, denominator: ", X, Y
6 →    PRINT X; "/"; Y; "="; FNDivide(X, Y)
```

One-line functions can often be too restrictive to be of any real use in a program. Suppose that a function needs to make a decision about the arguments before calculating the result. You should use the block DEF FN statement because it lets you define functions in much the same way you define subroutines with SUB...END SUB. Here is an example:

1 Beginning a Function

To begin a block function definition, start with DEF FN followed by the name of the function and any arguments it should accept. This is like SUB...END SUB, except QBasic does not open up a new window for you to edit your function.

WHY WORRY?

Function Definitions

Do not put an equal symbol (=) after the function arguments. QBasic will think you want to define a regular, one-line FN function.

2 Defining the Function

After the beginning DEF FN statement, you can put any statements you want to define your function. For the FNDivide function, an IF...THEN statement checks for a zero denominator before performing the division. Just as with a subroutine, you can include any statements you want, including PRINT and INPUT.

3 Returning a Value

After your function has computed what it needs to compute, there needs to be a way to get the computation out of the function. QBasic has an easy way to do this: the result of the function is set by assigning a value to the function name. In this case, the statement FNDivide = Num / Den makes the result of the function equal to the quotient of Num and Den.

4 Jumping Out of the Function

Sometimes you might need to leave the body of the function prematurely. EXIT DEF enables you to quit the function immediately. If no result was set, the result of the function is zero. However, you can set a result, and when QBasic performs the EXIT DEF, it keeps that result.

5 Ending a Function

For QBasic to recognize the end of your function definition, the definition must be followed by the END DEF statement.

6 Using the Function

The block DEF FN statement defines a function that can be used just like the one-line DEF FN statement. Although the block DEF FN statement lets you include statements in the function definition, you still cannot use the function where a statement should appear. If FNPrint is a function that prints the argument, you cannot have a line in your program that says FNPrint("Hello!") by itself.

LESSON 35

Subroutines that Give Something Back

```
' The main routine
CALL Menu.Action(Menu.Choice%)

SUB Menu.Action(I%)
    SELECT CASE I%
    CASE 1
        PRINT "Action #1"
    CASE 2
        PRINT "Action #2"
    CASE ELSE
        PRINT "What?"
    END SELECT
END SUB

FUNCTION Menu.Choice%()
    CALL Menu.Display
    INPUT Choice%
    Menu.Choice% = Choice%
END FUNCTION

SUB Menu.Display
    PRINT "   Le Menu!   "
    PRINT "1. Choice #1"
    PRINT "2. Choice #2"
    PRINT "3. Choice #3 (quit)"
END SUB
```

Having the `FN` as part of the function name can be distracting. The program in the previous lesson would have been easier to read if the function were `Divide` rather than `FNDivide`. The `FUNCTION...END FUNCTION` statement lets you define functions in much the same way, but without the obtrusive `FN`.

1 The Main Routine

The main routine is where QBasic begins execution when you start your program. The main routine in this lesson is simple, precise, and very understandable. Because QBasic has easy-to-use subroutines and functions, you should try to break your programming ideas into components that fit into these structures, as this menu program shows.

2 Starting a Function

To start a function, type in the FUNCTION statement followed by the subroutine name and any arguments. As soon as you press the Enter key, QBasic clears the screen and puts the cursors between the FUNCTION statement you entered and an END FUNCTION. Your main routine is not gone; press F2. Every function or subroutine you create with SUB...END SUB and FUNCTION...END FUNCTION appears in this listing. To get back to the main routine, highlight Untitled, and press Enter.

3 Arguments

The arguments you give to functions defined with FUNCTION...END FUNCTION are exactly like the arguments for subroutines and DEF FN functions. You must use arguments when you want to pass information to the function.

4 Jumping Out of the Function

If you need to leave the function prematurely, EXIT FUNCTION makes QBasic skip to the END FUNCTION statement. EXIT FUNCTION behaves exactly like EXIT DEF from the previous lesson.

5 Ending a Function

The END FUNCTION statement tells QBasic you are finished with the definition of the function and are ready to give the result. Every function must have an END FUNCTION statement.

6 Using the Function

Functions defined with FUNCTION...END FUNCTION can be used like functions defined with DEF FN. The only exception is that the function name does not have to begin with FN. As before, even though functions defined this way can contain statements, they cannot be used by themselves in place of a statement.

Reserved words   Identifiers and symbols   Strings and numbers   Comments

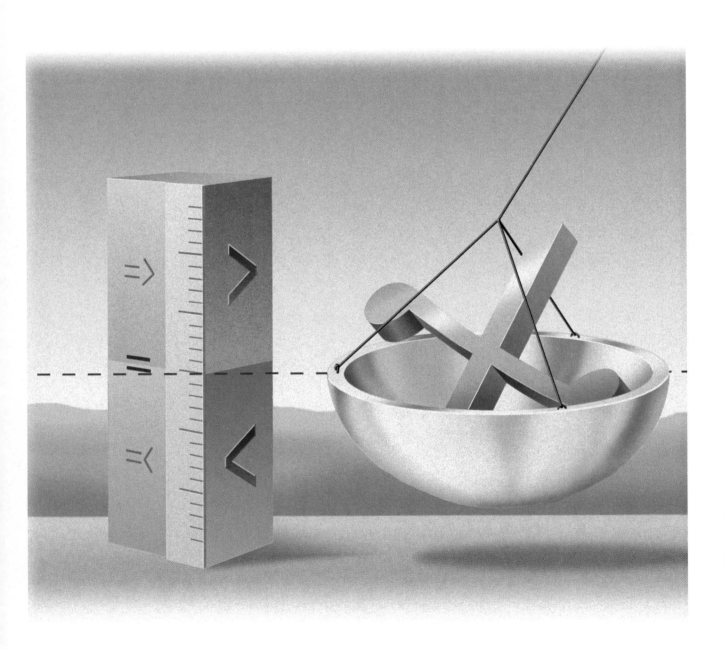

PART 6

Mathematics

Computers are especially good at number crunching. Unlike humans, computers can perform millions of complex calculations quickly and accurately. QBasic enables you to tap the power of your computer to process numbers with its impressive collection of mathematical operators and functions.

Using QBasic Math

QBasic can do everything that most calculators and adding machines can do. You can add, subtract, multiply, and divide numbers. Fortunately, getting QBasic to do math is easy, because the way you tell QBasic to calculate something is much like the way you key in a calculation on your calculator or adding machine.

For example, to add 1.25 and 3.15 on a calculator, you punch in 1.25 and hit the *plus* key. Then you punch in 3.15. The *equals* key finishes things up and gives you the answer of 4.4.

You can do the same calculation in QBasic in almost exactly the same way. In QBasic, you first type PRINT to make QBasic generate some output, and then you type 1.25 + 3.15. When QBasic executes this statement, it displays 4.4 on your screen, just as you would hope.

QBasic has many extra features that most pocket calculators don't have, like *variables*, not to mention other features like graphics and sound. Variables and the special mathematical functions enable you to perform complicated calculations with great ease and accuracy. But the freedom to handle the added complexity has its problems.

36 Setting a Precedent

37 More or Less Mathematics

38 Multiplication

39 Fun with Fractions

40 Giving the Computer the Third Degree

41 A Reminder...Remainder

42 Rounding

43 Random Number Generation RND...

44 Seeing the Signs

Calculations versus Expressions

Calculations in QBasic are called mathematical expressions, or *expressions* for short. Why not just call them *calculations* and be done with it? You could, but a subtle yet important difference exists between expressions and calculations. A calculation has a definite result. You punch the calculation into your calculator and get the answer, and unless you made mistakes in the process, the answer is right for the calculation.

But now suppose that you need to know X + 1.5, where X is a variable. What is the answer? Without knowing the value of X, you have nothing here to calculate. Of course, after you know a value for X, you can calculate X + 1.5; just replace X with the value it represents and continue. But when X doesn't stand for anything in particular, X + 1.5 only expresses a calculation.

Understanding Precedence

Mathematical expressions can sometimes be quite complex, with many operations in one expression. Even simple expressions can cause problems of interpretation. For example, if you ask QBasic to calculate 20 - 10 - 5, how should it interpret this calculation? Should QBasic compute 20 - 10 first, then subtract 5 to give 5? Or should QBasic do the 10 - 5 part first, then subtract the result from 20, giving 15?

Worse still, how about 1 / 2 + 1? If you add 2 + 1 first, you get 0.3333... , but if you do 1 / 2 before the addition, you get 1.5.

Fortunately, you don't need to worry about what part of a calculation QBasic does first because of a set of rules called *operator precedence*. Operator precedence tells QBasic that, by convention, certain calculations must be done before others. One rule says that QBasic always does multiplication and

division before addition and subtraction. Therefore, the preceding example 1 / 2 + 1 always gives 1.5 because QBasic must perform the division before the addition. The calculation 1 + 1 / 2 also gives 1.5 for the same reason.

What about 20 - 10 - 5? QBasic has an easy way to handle this type of expression: it always evaluates an expression from left to right. When QBasic sees the expression 20 - 10 - 5, it works on the 20 - 10 part first. Next, QBasic uses that result to finish computing the expression. 20 - 10 gives 10. 10 - 5 gives 5. With this rule, you always know how QBasic is going to evaluate any expression you give it.

Changing Precedence

Sometimes you need to change how QBasic evaluates an expression. What if you really want 1 / 2 + 1 to come out to 0.333...? QBasic enables you to insert parentheses around the parts of an expression you want to calculate first. Parentheses have precedence over all the other rules. Looking back at the example, 1 / (2 + 1) makes QBasic evaluate the 2 + 1 part before it does the division.

QBasic does anything in parentheses first. After that, exponents have precedence. Then come multiplication and division, which are given equal weight. Addition and subtraction are next, to which QBasic also gives equal importance. Remember, though, that QBasic always evaluates from left to right. So even though multiplication and division have equal precedence, the expression 1 / 2 * 2 results in 1.

Using Different Data Types

The mathematical operators you use in QBasic do not care what kind of numbers you are calculating, as long as they are, in fact, numbers. In Part 2, you read about the data types QBasic uses, such as single- and double-precision floating-point numbers and integers. When QBasic is calculating an expression, it uses the most precise data type in the expression to hold the result. Suppose that you add two integers. The result is computed as an integer. But if you add an integer and a double-precision number, the result is computed as a double-precision number.

This fact has important implications that you can read about in the following text of this part.

Computing by Lottery

Depending on what kind of program you are writing, you may want your program to do something unexpected. An accounting program that picks your year-end balance at random would be ridiculous. But what about games? A computer game that always does the same thing may get to be quite boring! QBasic has a function called RND that essentially lets your programs draw numbers from a hat and make decisions on those arbitrary values.

Exploring Other Functions

QBasic supports many other mathematical functions. The lessons in this Part cover only a few of them to whet your appetite, but the knowledge you gain should help you discover the rest of the functions QBasic has to offer you.

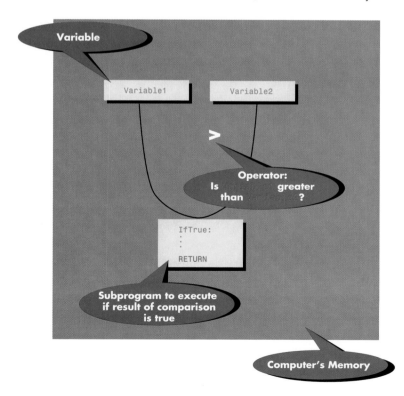

LESSON 36

Setting a Precedent

```
1 ──▶ PRINT (10 + 20) / 30      ' Where do I begin...
2 ──▶ PRINT 2 ^ 2               ' Power up!
3 ──▶ PRINT 1 + 7 * 2 / 3 \ 3   ' What is this mess?
4 ──▶ PRINT 4 * 2 MOD 6 / 2     ' What's left...
  ──▶ PRINT 20 - 10 - 5         ' Not this again!
5
```

This lesson lets you experiment with examples to understand the precedence rules that QBasic imposes.

Type the next program and start it if you like. Read the explanations carefully to understand what is going on.

1 Parentheses First

The precedence rules that QBasic imposes say that an expression in parentheses has precedence over the operators next to it. In other words, the expression inside a pair of parentheses, however complex the expression may be, should be treated like one number.

2 Exponents Next

The exponentiation operator ^ gets the next level of precedence. What would you expect QBasic to compute if you changed this line to PRINT 2 ^ 2 ^ 4? Remember, whenever precedence rules are not enough for QBasic to figure out what to do, it evaluates an expression from left to right. Try inserting parentheses in different places to see what happens.

3 Multiplication and Division

The next operations that QBasic considers when evaluating an expression are multiplication and division, including integer division with the operator \. How would you make this line compute 1 / 6 rather than 3 / 2?

4 Remainders

The MOD operator is like division, but it computes the remainder after division. You will read about this operator later, but all you need to know now is that this operator sits between division and addition in terms of precedence.

5 Addition and Subtraction

Lowest on the totem pole for mathematical operators are addition and subtraction. QBasic performs these operations last.

Order of Operations

QBasic does not really hunt through your expression to find the first set of parentheses to calculate, then the first exponentiations, and so on. QBasic uses the rule of left to right. Only when QBasic comes to a part of the expression where precedence rules are necessary to decipher the expression does QBasic use them.

For example, when QBasic evaluates the expression 1 + 2 + 3 * 6 + 9, the result is 30. QBasic first adds 1 + 2. When QBasic gets to the next part of the expression, the rules of precedence take over; it performs the multiplication before the addition. So QBasic computes 3 * 6 to get 18. You have no more problems here because the next thing to do is an addition. But QBasic still had to put off one addition, so next it adds 3 and 18. Finally, 9 is put into the sum, and out pops 30.

LESSON 37

More or Less Mathematics

```
1    X! = 32767          ' A single-precision...
     Y# = 1              ' ...meets a double-
                           precision...
2    Z = X! + Y#         ' ...and get stuck back
                           as double-precision

3
     PRINT 32766 + 1     ' These are just integers
4    PRINT 32768 + 1     ' But this is a long integer
                           and an integer!

5    X = 32767! + 1        ' Singles and integers
                             won't overflow
```

Addition and subtraction are easy to do in QBasic. QBasic defines the two symbols + and - to act as operators that make QBasic add or subtract.

Look over this sample program, and read on:

1 Variables

Mathematical expressions can contain both numeric constants and numeric variables. In fact, the variables are what make an expression more than just a calculation. QBasic is just as happy adding or subtracting variables as it is constants.

2 Adding Different Data Types

QBasic does not mind if you mingle data types in your expressions. For example, you can add an integer and a single-precision number, like the preceding sample program does. However, QBasic first converts the integer to a single-precision number before doing the addition to keep the result as accurate as possible.

3 Overflow

When QBasic stops your program and tells you that an *overflow* has occurred, the calculation QBasic performed has exceeded the range of the data type with which it was working. Remember that QBasic performs calculations in the most precise data type. The expression `32767 + 1#` is a sum of an integer and a double-precision number, so QBasic converts the 32767 to a double-precision number.

4 Long Integers

Long integers take up twice as much memory as regular integers, but they also can operate in a much larger range. This expression does not overflow because QBasic recognizes that 32768 is a long integer; it cannot fit in the range of regular integers. When this expression is evaluated, 1 is converted to a long integer before the calculation.

5 Single Precision

Calculations can overflow, but QBasic also can let you know about overflows when you try to store a result that is out of range for that type of variable. In an earlier step you saw how to calculate `32767 + 1` without getting the result to overflow. Try changing the variable on this line into an integer variable. Remember that QBasic views variables with a `%` after them as integer variables.

Reserved words   Identifiers and symbols   Strings and numbers   Comments

LESSON 38
Multiplication

```
2  ──► DEF FNAdjustSalary(Sal, OTRate, OT) = Sal + ⟲
          OTRate * OT
4  ─────┘
       ──► INPUT "Enter salary, OT  rate and OT: ", ⟲
1  ───►   Sal, OTRate, OT
       ──► PRINT USING "Adjusted salary is
3  ───► **$##,.##."; FNAdjustSalary(Sal, OTRate, OT) ⟲
```

Multiplication is just as easy to perform as addition and subtraction in QBasic. The following program uses multiplication to compute overtime for a salaried employee:

1 Two Lines?

The main module of this sample program has only two lines. The first line uses the INPUT statement to get the salary, overtime rate, and overtime hours for an employee. The next line prints out the result with PRINT USING. The heart of the program is in a function defined earlier in the program.

2 DEF FN

Remember that DEF FN is one of the ways that QBasic enables you to define functions. DEF FN is useful for creating functions, especially mathematical functions, that are usually just one line long.

3 USING

The format string in this example leaves six spaces for printing out the adjusted salary, plus two decimal digits. The , (comma) before the decimal point tells QBasic to insert commas into the integer part of the number. The format string also uses the floating asterisks and dollar sign. This way, a dollar sign always appears before the number, and * fills up the unused space.

4 Precedence

Remember that the multiplication operator * has a higher precedence than +. QBasic performs the multiplication before the addition, and the adjusted salary makes sense.

LESSON 39

Fun with Fractions

```
       ' A Bogus calculation
  10      INPUT "Number please: ", N#
        V% = 1 / ((N# - 1) * (N# + 1))
        PRINT "The result of 1 / (("; N#; "- 1) * (";
        PRINT N#; " + 1)) fairly close to"; V%; "."

  20      INPUT "How about two more: ", N%, M%
        PRINT N%; "divided by"; M%; "is"; N% / M%;
        PRINT "(or about"; N% \ M%; ")."
        END
```

1

2

3

Division needs special care. Type the next program and try using 1 when it asks for input.

1 Division by Zero

The denominator of a fraction cannot be zero. If you try to divide a number by zero, QBasic stops your program and gives you a `Division By Zero` error. Before performing a division, always check that the denominator is not zero. Add a line to this program to tell the user to enter a value that doesn't make the denominator zero.

2 Data Types

Recall that QBasic always performs mathematical operations in the most precise type that is being calculated. This method does not make much sense if you are dividing two integers, like `7 / 2`, because the fraction is

discarded if the division is performed with just integers. For division, QBasic always converts to single- or double-precision numbers first. However, you still can store the result in an integer variable.

3 Integer Division

You can make QBasic perform division using integers by typing the backwards division symbol `\`, also called the *backslash*. With this operator, QBasic converts the numbers you divide to integers *first*, then it performs the calculation, rounding if necessary. For example, `11.2 \ 4` is 2, but `11.5 \ 4` is 3 because of rounding.

104

Standard Division

In standard division, the result is usually a double. If both operands are integers or single expressions, the result is a single unless it overflows, in which case, the result is a double.

Integer Division

Before integer division is performed, the operands are rounded to integers or long data types. Usually, the data type of the resulting value is an integer or a long regardless of whether the result is a whole number. Any fractional portion of the resulting value is truncated.

Giving the Computer the Third Degree

```
1 ──────► INPUT "Enter a number and an exponent, separated
              by commas: ", A, B
              PRINT A; "raised to the power of"; B; "is ";
3 ──────► PRINT USING "#.#####^^^^"; A ^ B ◄────── 4
```

Exponents are sometimes used to indicate a repeated multiplication, like 3 * 3 * 3. The next sample program demonstrates some of the uses of the exponentiation operator:

1 Data Types

Exponentiation always gives you single- or double-precision numbers as a result. When you use the exponentiation operator, you can sometimes get extremely large numbers. Always be sure to check for an overflow if you plan on storing the result of this operator in an integer variable.

2 Precedence

The exponentiation operator has the highest precedence of all the mathematical operators.

3 Scientific Notation

When you use the exponentiation operator, you can often end up with numbers that are extremely large or small. Therefore, you should use scientific notation when you need to use extremely large or small numbers in your program. When you want to display numbers in scientific notation, you can use the special character ^ in a PRINT USING format string. This character was not covered in the section on input and output because it is not often used.

The ^ character is easy to use in a format string. You can put four or five of them after the hash symbols that tell QBasic to display a number.

4 Overflow

You can very easily reach the limits of the data types that QBasic supports with the exponentiation operator. Try running this program and give it 100 and 200 as input. Even these small numbers overshoot the limits of the double-precision data type.

A Reminder...Remainder

```
1      PRINT 7 MOD 3
2      PRINT 2 * 7 MOD 3 + 1
       ' Is this 3 or 2? Remember precedence!

3      PRINT 8 MOD 3, 7.5 MOD 3, 7.2 MOD 3

       PRINT 32770 * 32767.5 MOD 32767.5        4
```

The MOD operator evaluates the remainder of an integer division like 10 \ 7. This program demonstrates the operation of MOD:

1 Remainders

MOD computes the remainder after division of the number on the left of the MOD operator by the number on the right. For example, 7 MOD 3 evaluates to 1.

2 Precedence

A few lessons ago, you read about the precedence of the MOD operator. MOD is between the precedence of multiplication and division and the precedence of addition and subtraction.

3 Rounding Off Fractions

The MOD operator works only with integers or long integers. The MOD operator computes the remainder after dividing numbers like 7.8 and 3 by rounding the floating-point number to an integer then computing the result.

4 Which Type?

The result of the MOD operator is computed in the type of the number on the right of the operator, after the number has been rounded to an integer or a long integer. Try changing this line from a PRINT statement to an assignment statement that stores the result of the calculation in an integer variable. Change the variable to a long integer variable and see what happens.

LESSON 42

Rounding

```
' Use two kinds of rounding to see the difference
INPUT "Give a number to round, please: ", X
PRINT X; "truncated is"; FIX(X)
PRINT X; "rounded is"; INT(X)

' The next line could give you an overflow
K% = X
PRINT X; "rounded (what QBasic does normally) is";
K%
```

1

2

3

4

You have seen how rounding takes place when QBasic needs to convert numbers before a calculation. If the way that QBasic rounds fractions is not the way you want, you can tell QBasic explicitly how to round. This program is a good example.

1 Truncation

You can use several ways to round numbers to fit into an integer. The method you choose depends on the application. For example, in some forms of accounting, it is better to lose a penny. A number like 100.5 or 100.8 should round to 100, not to 101 like QBasic normally chooses. This kind of rounding is called *truncation*, and QBasic can easily use this method with the FIX function. FIX simply chops off the fractional part of a number and leaves an integer.

2 Normal Rounding

The traditional way to round numbers is to pick the closest whole number. For example, 100.2 should round to 100, and -100.7 should round to -101. What should you do with 3.5 and -3.5? QBasic chooses to round these numbers to 4 and -4, respectively. This technique is the way QBasic rounds numbers normally, but you can also do so explicitly with the INT function.

3 Loss of Precision

Always try to store data in a variable that has the most precision for the information you are keeping. It doesn't make much sense to keep gas mileage in an integer because the quantity has a fractional part. When you discard the fractional part, you lose valuable information about the number. Round numbers when necessary, but be careful that you are not throwing away a fraction you need.

4 Overflow

This statement can cause problems. Remember that QBasic generates an
Overflow Error if you try to store a value that is outside the range
allowed for the data type of some variable. But FIX and INT never
overflow. These functions don't return integers but rather single- or
double-precision numbers with the fractional part removed.

However, you cannot use FIX or INT to store a value like 32,769 in an
integer variable. Neither FIX(32769) nor INT(32769) will generate an
overflow, but I% = FIX(32769) will; 32769 is *still* outside the integer
range.

Random Number Generation
RND

```
        RANDOMIZE 40

1 ►     PRINT RND(-1); RND(1)
        PRINT RND(-1); RND(1); RND(1)
3       PRINT RND(-1); RND(1); RND(1); RND(1)

        PRINT RND(1); RND(0); RND(1); RND(0)
```

2

Random variations are the spice of life. The sample program for this lesson shows you how to add a little extra life to your programs.

Type this program now, then read on to see what it is all about.

1 Inciting Chaos

The QBasic function RND gets a value from something called a *pseudorandom number generator*. A pseudorandom number generator generates numbers one at a time within some range, say between 0 and 1. The numbers appear randomly. In other words, if you look at the numbers you get from the generator, they have no apparent order to them.

WHAT DOES IT MEAN?

Pseudo is a Greek word for *false*, so a pseudo-random number generator is a *false random number generator*. A subprogram inside QBasic spits out a random number based on a number called a *seed*. The generator calculates a random number based on the last one it gave you. If you start the generator in the same place each time, you will get the same sequence of numbers.

RND actually takes a numeric argument. If the argument is greater than 0, RND generates a new random number between 0 and 1 and returns it to you. You can get the last random number that was generated by sending RND an argument of 0.

2 Seeding

By now you should be aware of the fact that the RND function does not give you truly random values. If you are writing a game based on this function, your audience may quickly tire of the computer taking the same course of action every time!

Remember that the part of QBasic that generates the values returned by RND is based on a special number called the *seed*. In QBasic, you can give a seed value with the RANDOMIZE statement. In this lesson, RANDOMIZE 40 changes the seed to the value of 40.

3 Starting Over

RND(-1) makes the QBasic random number generator go back to the first random number it generated since the last RANDOMIZE statement. Each time you call RND(-1), the sequence of random numbers you get is repeated. In fact, if you look carefully at the output of the sample program for this lesson, you can see that this repeated sequence is exactly what happens.

WHY WORRY?

If you give RND a value that is less than zero, something interesting happens: RND starts the sequence of random numbers it has been generating from the top.

LESSON 44

Seeing the Signs

```
        INPUT "Enter the first number: ", F
        INPUT "Enter the last number: ", L

        IF F = L THEN END

        FOR I% = F TO L STEP SGN(L - F)
            J = ABS(I%)
            K = SQR(J)

            PRINT "The square root of "; I%; " is ";
            IF SGN(I%) < 0 THEN
                    PRINT K; "i"
            ELSE
                    PRINT K
            END IF
        NEXT I%
```

1

2

3

4

This Part concludes by looking at a few more QBasic mathematical functions: SGN, ABS, and SQR. The following program looks like it may contain an error, but it doesn't. Read carefully to see why.

1 Assigning Signs to Values

When you start this program, QBasic asks you for a first number and a last number. The program prints out the square roots of all the whole numbers, starting with the first number and ending with the last, using a FOR...NEXT loop.

WHY WORRY?

Remember that the FOR statement looks like FOR I = A TO B. If A is greater than B, the FOR loop does not execute because it doesn't have any work to do.

This program uses a FOR...STEP...NEXT loop, though, which tells QBasic to increase the loop variable by the step amount each time through the loop. The trick is to make the step amount -1 if the loop variable needs to count down and 1 if it needs to count up.

QBasic has a function that can help figure out the step amount. This function, SGN, takes an expression and returns -1 if the expression is less than zero, 1 if it is greater than zero, and 0 if it is exactly zero.

If the first number is less than the last number, the step amount needs to be 1— `SGN(L - F)` will be 1, the step amount that you need. However, if the first number is greater than the last, the step amount needs to be -1— `SGN(L - F)` returns the right step amount.

2 Fixing a Possible Bug

What happens if the first and last numbers are the same? `SGN(L - F)` returns 0 because `L - F` is 0. This number is no good as a `STEP` value. Try removing this line, the first `IF` statement, from the program and see what happens.

3 Square Root

`SQR` stands for square root, which is what this function calculates. In fact, this sample program prints out the square roots of all the integers between two numbers you enter.

Like most calculators, though, QBasic does not understand how to take the square root of negative numbers. Mathematicians invented a special class of numbers, called imaginary numbers, so that taking the square root of a number like -27.23 makes sense. QBasic has a limited imagination, so imaginary numbers are left up to you.

To be sure that `SQR` does not get any negative numbers, you need a way to discard the sign of a number.

4 Absolutely Positive

Mathematicians define the *absolute value* of a number as the positive distance of the number from 0. The `ABS` function calculates this value, but as far as QBasic is concerned, the absolute value of a number is just the number with a positive sign. For example, `ABS(-27.23)` is 27.23 and `ABS(42)` is 42.

The sample program for this lesson uses `ABS` to ensure that `SQR` never tries to take the square root of negative numbers.

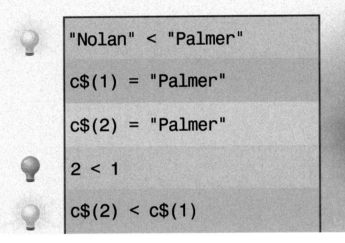

```
"Nolan" < "Palmer"

c$(1) = "Palmer"

c$(2) = "Palmer"

2 < 1

c$(2) < c$(1)
```

PART 7

Strings and String Manipulation

A *string* is a sequence of characters that occupy a chunk of your computer's memory. You have seen and used string constants and variables in previous lessons. For example, when you use the statement `PRINT "Hello, "; UserName$` in your program to greet the user, you are using strings to hold English words and names.

The fact that QBasic enables you to manipulate character strings makes them one of the most powerful features of the BASIC programming language. Even with the limit that QBasic imposes on the length of character strings (32,767 characters), you can do many things that QBasic would otherwise not allow or know how to do.

Building Character Strings

Because you are in complete control of the character strings in your program, you need to build them up to contain the information you want. QBasic gives you the ability to put smaller strings together by a process called *concatenation*. When you tell QBasic to concatenate two strings, QBasic creates a new string by combining the two smaller ones.

For example, if you tell QBasic to concatenate `"Doe"`, `","` and `"John J."`, you get the string `"Doe, John J."`. QBasic doesn't bother interpreting what any of these strings mean. Only the computer must understand what is going on.

45 Simple String Building

46 Searching for Substrings in a String

47 Character Codes and Numeric Strings

48 Do You Have the Time?

49 More String-Building Functions

But if you want your character strings to mean something, you need to be able to break apart the strings you build to get at whatever information you need. For example, suppose that you have stored the user's name in a string variable as the character string `"L=User,F=Ulysses,M=A"`, but you need to get to just the first name. You have no way to get to the first name by concatenating strings.

As you may guess, QBasic gives you a powerful set of functions for dissecting strings. These smaller pieces that comprise your string are called *substrings*. `LEFT$` creates a substring from the beginning of a string. For example, `LEFT$("L=User,F=Ulysses,M=A", 6)` gives you the string `"L=User"`. Another function, `RIGHT$`, creates a substring from the end of a string. But by far the most powerful function that QBasic gives you for manipulating strings is the `MID$` function. `MID$` is discussed in more detail in the first lesson. This figure shows how these functions operate on a particular string.

Looking for that Special Substring

`LEFT$`, `RIGHT$`, and `MID$` are enough to allow you to handle strings for nearly every task you can imagine doing. But some things you may like to do with character strings can get downright ugly if you use just these three functions.

Remember Mr. User from the preceding section? His first name is still trapped inside the string `"L=User,F=Ulysses,M=A"`. You know that the substring `"Ulysses"` starts at the 10th character in this string and continues on for seven characters. Well, `RIGHT$("L=User,F=Ulysses,M=A", 11)` gives you the string `"Ulysses,M=A"`, and `LEFT$("Ulysses,M=A", 7)` gives you `"Ulysses"`, so you *can* get at Mr. User's first name.

More importantly, the way you went about getting at his name will not always work. Suppose you want to find Ms. Doe's first name. Her name is trapped somewhere in the string `"L=Doe,F=Jane,M=B"`. If you perform exactly the same steps,

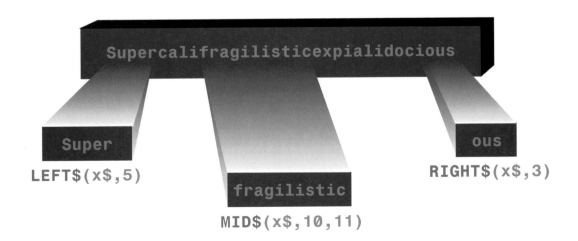

`RIGHT$("L=Doe,F=Jane,M=B", 11)`
gives you `",F=Jane,M=B"` and
`LEFT$(",F=Jane,M=B", 7)` gives you
`",F=Jane"`. Ms. Doe's first name is not likely
to be ,F=Jane!

Nevertheless, you know how to find the
name in the string. First names start with
the string `"F="` and go on to the next
comma in the string. If only you had a way
to search through a string to find a
particular substring...

You do! The `INSTR` function looks in a string
for a particular substring. If `INSTR` finds the
string you are looking for, the function
returns the number of the substring's place
in the character string. For example,
`INSTR("L=User,F=Ulysses,M=A", "F=")`
returns 8 because the substring `"F="` starts at
the eighth character in this string. You can
learn much more about `INSTR` in
Lesson 46.

Adding Numbers Inside Strings

Suppose that you decide to put salaries
inside the strings we have been discussing
so far. Mr. User makes $38,500 each year,
and you want his string to look like
`"L=User,F=Ulysses,M=A,S=38500"`. You
know how to tack the `","` and the `"S="`
onto the string `"L=User,F=Ulysses,M=A"`,
but how about the salary, assuming that the
salary is stored in a numeric variable like
`Salary`?

QBasic has a handy way to convert numbers
into strings and strings into numbers. The
`STR$` function enables you to give it any kind

of number, and the function gives you back a
string representing that number in decimal.
For example, `STR$(Salary)` returns `" 38500"`
for Mr. User. You can go the other way, too,
and convert a string representing
a number into a number with the `VAL`
function. `VAL("-38500")` gives you `-38500`.

You can use another way to convert special
numbers into strings: *character codes*.

Using Character Codes

The characters in a string are stored as a
sequence of bytes in a chunk of your computer's memory. When a string is displayed
on-screen, the computer needs to figure out
what character is represented by each byte of
the string. In most computers, the string
`"ABC"` is stored as the sequence of bytes 65,
66, and 67. These numbers are the *ASCII*
values of the characters; `"A"` is 65, `"B"` is 66,
and `"C"` is 67. The *American Standards
Committee for Information Interchange* has
established universal numeric values that
represent all characters. This figure shows the
difference between the string you see and the
string the computer sees.

Sometimes you may need to put special
characters into your strings, but the QBasic
editor normally does not allow special
characters.

QBasic does not leave you out in the cold!
The function `CHR$` enables you to convert an
ASCII code (character code) into a string
with the corresponding character in it. If you
don't have a chart of the ASCII character set,
you can generate one in Lesson 47.

Simple String Building

```
        ' Use concatenation to build a long word
   10   INPUT "Gimme a word        : ", word1$
        INPUT "Gimme another word : ", word2$
1 ───►  word$ = word1$ + word2$

        PRINT "Your word is: "; CHR$(34); word$; CHR$(34); ↵
        "..."
   20   PRINT "Enter a number from 1 to "; LEN(word$); ": "; ↵
        INPUT X1%
2 ───►  PRINT "LEFT$ = "; CHR$(34); LEFT$(word$, X1%); ↵
        CHR$(34)
3 ───►  PRINT "RIGHT$ = "; CHR$(34); RIGHT$(word$, X1%); ↵
        CHR$(34)
4 ───►  PRINT "MID$ = "; CHR$(34); MID$(word$, X1%); ↵
        CHR$(34)
```

In this lesson you can explore some of the simple string building functions that QBasic provides.

Type the following program, and we will examine the important details of it next.

1 Concatenating Strings

QBasic makes concatenation a snap by giving the addition operator + a special meaning for character strings. When you add two character strings, you tell QBasic to concatenate them. QBasic willingly joins the strings and returns the combined string.

In this loop, the program asks the user to enter a word. The first word is stored in word1$ while the second is stored in word2$. Both variables are then concatenated and stored into the variable word$.

2 Extracting Characters from the Left Part of a String

LEFT$ is a function that takes two arguments. The first argument is a character string constant or a string variable, and the second argument is an integer. LEFT$ returns a new string consisting of the left part of the input string, and the integer argument specifies how many characters to put into the new string. For example, LEFT$("Test String", 3) returns "Tes".

3 Extracting Characters from the Right Part of a String

RIGHT$ is a function that behaves much like LEFT$. RIGHT$ takes the same number and type of arguments as LEFT$. The only difference is that RIGHT$ returns a new string consisting of rightmost characters of the string argument. See what happens when you type RIGHT$("Test String", 3) and RIGHT$("A", 10) using your program.

4 Extracting Characters from the Middle of a String

MID$ is an extremely powerful function. Like LEFT$ and RIGHT$, the MID$ function has a string constant or string variable as its first argument and an integer argument as the second. MID$ also takes an optional integer as the third argument.

The MID$ function returns a new string consisting of a portion of the string argument, beginning somewhere within the string. Starting with 1 as the first character of the string, the second argument tells MID$ where to start looking. The example of MID$ in the preceding program uses only two arguments, meaning MID$ should return all the characters from the starting position to the end of the string.

MID$("Test String", 3) returns "st String", for example, and MID$("A", 10) also works, but this example returns the *empty string* because nothing is after the first character position.

> **WHAT DOES IT MEAN?**
>
> The *empty string* is just a character string with no characters in it, and it looks like " ".

5 MID$ with Three Arguments

You can give a third argument to the MID$ function. This argument tells QBasic to limit the number of characters it puts into the new string. If you ask for MID$("Test String", 3, 2) you get the string "st". How about MID$("Test String", 3, 100) or MID$("A", 10, 1)? Try these examples and see.

> **WHY WORRY?**
>
> Sometimes QBasic reports an Illegal Function Call, meaning that an argument to the function just called was not right for some reason. The integer arguments to LEFT$, RIGHT$, and MID$ cannot be negative nor can the arguments point beyond the end of a string, QBasic reports this situation as an error.

Reserved words   Identifiers and symbols   Strings and numbers   Comments

LESSON 46

Searching for Substrings in a String

```
LINE INPUT "Enter Account: "; N$

' Pull out the First, Last and Middle from the
  account
PRINT "First Name: "; Fld$(N$, "F")
PRINT "Last Name: "; Fld$(N$, "L")
PRINT "Middle Initial: "; Fld$(N$, "M")

' A generic function for extracting fields...
FUNCTION Fld$(N$, F$)
    I% = INSTR(N$, F$ + "=")
    IF I% = 0  THEN
            Fld$ = ""
    ELSE
        J% = INSTR(I%, N$, ",")
        IF J% = 0 THEN J% = LEN(N$) + 1
        Fld$ = MID$(N$, I% + 2, J% - I% - 2)
    END IF
END FUNCTION
```

The following program looks complicated, but it isn't. When the program asks for an account, enter a string like `"L=User,F=Ulysses,M=A"`.

1 The Fld$ Function

In the introduction of this Part, you looked at character strings that held a person's name in a manner like `"L=Grant,M=G,F=Golly"`. We hinted at using INSTR to break a string like this apart to find the first name, but here is where the fun starts.

The Fld$ function takes a string, like `"L=Grant,M=G,F=Golly"`, and another string telling Fld$ what information you want. `"F"`, for example, gets you the first name from the string. If QBasic can find the information you want, Fld$ returns that information. Otherwise, you get an empty string back.

2 INSTR from the Start

Remember that INSTR searches through a string to find the first occurrence of a substring. In this example, INSTR looks through the variable N$ for the string F$ + "=".

N$ holds a string like `"L=Grant,M=G,F=Golly"`, and F$ holds the letter for one of the substrings in N$ you want to see. So you ask `INSTR` to look for a string like `"F="` in N$. Now, if `INSTR` returns 0, then the desired substring does not exist in N$ — thus the information you want is not there.

3 | INSTR **from Elsewhere**

`INSTR` lets you pass an integer argument before the two strings. This integer tells `INSTR` to start looking at some character in the middle of the string, not from the beginning. For example, `INSTR("a-ab-abc", "b")` returns 4, but `INSTR(5, "a-ab-abc", "b")` returns 7 because the first time that `INSTR` sees `"b"` after the fifth character in `"a-ab-abc"` is at the seventh character.

Suppose that you call `Fld$` with `"L=Grant,M=G,F=Golly"` and `"M"`. The first `INSTR` sets I% to 9, because the ninth position is where the first `"M="` begins. Imagine that this line is change to `J% = INSTR(N$, ",")`. J% would be set to 8. But we are going to use I% and J% to say *the information you want starts at position I% and goes on to position J%.* Constructed this way, the program wouldn't make sense. As the program is written, the statement `J% = INSTR(I%, N$, ",")` tells `INSTR` to look for the first comma after the `"M="`.

4 | **A Catch**

`INSTR` has one catch. Suppose that you call `Fld$` with `"L=Grant,M=G,F=Golly"` and `"F"` this time. The first `INSTR` sets I% to 13 like we want. However, J% is set to 0 because no `","` exists after the `"F="`.

5 | **Pulling Out the Stops**

The `Fld$` function is almost done. At this point, I% is set to the beginning of the string F$ + `"="`, and J% is set to the spot in the string where the comma should be. If the information is at the end of the string N$, no comma exists, but J% is set as if a comma existed.

To wrap up this function, you need to get `Fld$` to return the string of information between the F$ + `"="` part and the `","` part. The information you want starts at character position I% + 2 (you want to skip over the F$ + `"="` part). Identifying the length is the tricky step. The string has J% - I% + 1 characters between positions I% and J%. But you need to throw out three characters because you are skipping the F$ + `"="` and the `","`. Therefore, J% - I% - 2 characters remain in between.

Character Codes and Numeric Strings

```
        ' See if the user wants an ASCII Table
        PRINT "Do you need an ASCII table? "
10        A$ = UCASE$(INKEY$)
        IF A$ = "N" THEN GOTO 30
        IF A$ = "Y" THEN GOTO 20
        GOTO 10

        ' Print an ASCII Table
20        FOR I% = 0 TO 255
            N$ = RIGHT$("000" + MID$(STR$(I%), 2), 3)
            S$ = N$ + " " + CHR$(34) + CHR$(I%) +
            CHR$(34) + SPACE$(16)

            PRINT LEFT$(S$, 16);
        NEXT I%

        END

30        INPUT "Give me a number or string: ", A$

        PRINT "VAL("; CHR$(34); A$; CHR$(34); ") = ";
        VAL(A$)
        PRINT "ASC("; CHR$(34); A$; CHR$(34); ") = ";
        ASC(A$)
```

If you don't have a table of the ASCII character codes, this program can generate one for you. The program has two parts. Don't worry if it looks confusing; the major parts are easy, and we will break them down in detail.

1 Decision Making

The program first asks if you want to display an ASCII table. If you respond with a **Y**, the program jumps to line 20 to display the table otherwise, if you respond with an **N**, the program jumps to line 30 to display character codes for characters entered at the keyboard.

Recall from lesson 17 that `INKEY$` waits for input from the keyboard. By combining `INKEY$` with `UCASE$` the program waits for input from the keyboard then converts it to uppercase, via `UCASE$`.

2 Executing Loops

The code at line label 20 is executed if you enter a **Y** at the `INKEY$` query. This portion of the program uses a `FOR...NEXT` loop to print out all 256 ASCII characters. `CHR$` takes a numeric value between 0 and 255, generated by the `FOR...NEXT`, and returns the character equivalent of the code.

3 Padding and Justification

This line, `N$ = RIGHT$("000" + MID$(STR$(I%), 2), 3)`, right-justifies the character code and fills in (*pads*) the spaces to the left with 0s. All the numbers come out like `"000"` or `"251"`.

4 Converting Numbers to Strings

One thing peculiar about the STR$ function is that it leaves a space for a sign — plus or minus. For example, `STR$(1000)` gives you `"1000"`, but `STR$(-1000)` gives `"-1000"`. `MID$` prunes off that space since all character codes are positive and the sign has no use in the context.

5 Characters and ASCII Values

At this point, you use `CHR$` to place double quotes around a character as well as to print the character represented by the character code. `CHR$(34)` prints a quote while `CHR$(I%)` print the character represented by `I%`.

6 Strings and Numbers

If you enter **N** at the `INKEY$` query the second part of the program is executed which allows you to experiment with the `ASC` and `VAL` functions. `VAL` takes a string representation of a number and returns the corresponding numeric value.

7 Characters and ASCII Values

`ASC`, the opposite of `CHR$`, returns the numeric code of a character, between 0 and 255, passed to the function.

WHY WORRY?

VAL returns 0 if you give it the empty string `""`, but ASC generates an `Illegal Function Call` error.

WHY WORRY?

VAL reads as much of the string as it under-stands and returns the value of that string. For example, `VAL("hello")` is zero because `"hello"` does not contain any kind of numeric format that VAL understands. `VAL("2.14")` gives you 2.14. Try `VAL("3,148.12")`. Why does this string just return 3?

LESSON 48

Do You Have the Time?

```
' Print the current date and time
1   PRINT "Today is "; DATE$;
2   PRINT " at "; TIME$;
    PRINT "."

' See if the user wants to change the date...
3   INPUT "Enter a new date, or just hit enter: ",
    NewDATE$
    IF NewDATE$ <> "" THEN DATE$ = NewDATE$

' ...or the time.
4   INPUT "Now enter a new time, or just hit enter: ",
    NewTIME$
    IF NewTIME$ <> "" THEN TIME$ = NewTIME$
```

This program prints the current date and time then asks you to enter the new date and time. Be sure to read over the steps because QBasic likes to have the date and time in a special format.

1 Retrieving the System Date

DATE$ is a function that returns the current date stored in your computer clock. This function always returns a string that is 10 characters long. The date string looks like `"05-22-1994"` with the month, day, and year separated by dashes.

Because the string returned by DATE$ is always in this nice format, try modifying the program in this lesson so it prints the date like `"22/05/94"`. To help you along, what strings do

`LEFT$(DATE$, 2)`, `MID$(DATE$, 4, 2)`, and `RIGHT$(DATE$, 4)` give you?

WHY WORRY?

Remember that DATE$ and TIME$ are not strings. They are functions that return strings; therefore, DATE$ and TIME$ cannot appear in the list of variables to INPUT or READ.

2 Retrieving the System Time

TIME$ is another function like DATE$ except that TIME$ returns the current time stored in your computer's 24-hour clock. TIME$ always returns a string that is eight characters long and looks like `"10:52:15"`. 10:52 in the evening looks like `"22:52:43"` in the 24-hour clock.

Experiment with TIME$. Have the program lop off the seconds from the time. Also, try modifying the program in this lesson so it prints the time for a 12-hour clock. This task is tricky. Remember that VAL returns the number represented by a string, and STR$ returns the string that represents a number. For example, VAL(LEFT$(TIME$, 2)) gives you the hour as a number, and STR$(Hour% - 12) gives you a string.

3 Setting the Date

If you want to change the date stored in your computer, you can just assign the new date string to DATE$. But you must be sure that the date string you assign to DATE$ is in the same format that DATE$ returns. For example, QBasic stops your program and reports an Illegal Function Call if you try to change the date with a string like "January 1, 1995" or even "02-31-1990" because February never has 31 days.

Can you think of a way to make the program in this lesson check for the proper date format before making the change?

4 Setting the Time

Setting the time on your computer clock works the same way as setting the date. You just assign a string with the new time to TIME$. Once again, however, you must be sure that the string is in the proper format before you assign it to TIME$.

More String-Building Functions

```
LINE INPUT "A Word Please: ", A$

' Before and after pictures
PRINT "Before SpaceWatchers: "; CHR$(34);
A$; CHR$(34)
A$ = LTRIM$(RTRIM$(A$))
PRINT "After SpaceWatchers: "; CHR$(34);
A$; CHR$(34)

' Some more string fun before this part
comes to a close
PadLen% = (75 - LEN(A$)) \ 2

ALower$ = LCASE$(A$)
AUpper$ = UCASE$(A$)

PRINT "'"; STRING$(PadLen%, 62); ALower$;
STRING$(PadLen%, "<**"); "'"
PRINT "'"; SPACE$(PadLen%); AUpper$;
STRING$(PadLen%, " "); "'"
```

1

2

3

4

QBasic supports many more string functions. The following program covers some of these functions. The explanations describe each function in detail.

1 Trimming Extra Spaces

LTRIM$ and RTRIM$ are two handy functions that trim off spaces on the left or right of a string. Run this program and enter "   Hello" so that the word is surrounded by spaces. LINE INPUT does not discard spaces, so when you enter "Hello" like this, A$ contains some space

around the word. Take a look at the *before* and *after* outputs. The *after* output has all the spaces trimmed off. Run the program again, but give it something like "Hello   World". Notice that spaces not at the left or right of the string are not affected.

2 Upper and Lower Case Strings

LCASE$ and UCASE$ convert all the characters in a string to lowercase or uppercase. Most characters are not affected by these two functions, but the alphabet characters do change. For example, LCASE$("123") gives "123", but LCASE$("One, Two, Three") becomes "one, two, three".

Lesson 47 introduced UCASE$. Now, given what you know about MID$, why not write a program that properly capitalizes a sentence? Ignore proper names, but do take care of the first word in the sentence as well as the word *I*.

3 Padding with Specified Characters

STRING$ is an easy way to make a string that is just copies of a single character. In the preceding example, STRING$ is used in two ways. In the first use, you give STRING$ a length and character code, and STRING$ makes a string with the length you request containing nothing but characters with the given character code. For example, STRING$(10, 32) gives you a string with 10 spaces in it.

You also can give STRING$ a character string rather than a character code. STRING$ takes the first character from the string and makes however many copies you want. STRING$(10, "+-!") gives the string "++++++++++", even though you gave STRING$ the string "+-!".

Try writing a function that makes copies of whole strings, not just the first character.

4 Padding with Spaces

SPACE$ is a shortcut for STRING$ with spaces. The program you typed in Lesson 47 used SPACE$ to justify strings for printing.

PART 8

Sound and Graphics

In Part 3, you read about how QBasic handles input from and output to the user. The PRINT statement is one of the primary ways to send information from your program to the user. But sometimes the PRINT statement does not communicate enough information. Sound and graphics, even very basic sound and graphics, are easy ways to grab the user's attention.

50 Sound Off!

51 Making Music

52 Getting into Graphics

53 Plotting Points

54 Geometric Figures

55 Filling Figures

56 Turtle Graphics

Adding Sounds

The usual output routines that QBasic gives you for displaying numeric and string constants can take you only so far. By adding sound to your programs, you can introduce an entirely new level of communication with the person who uses your programs.

At the lowest level of noise making, QBasic enables you to generate simple beeps on the computer speaker. Beeps of different tones can mean different things. For example, low beeps that are sustained for a long time can mean an input error, as if the computer were saying "No….That's not quite right." Short, piercing beeps can warn the user that something is very wrong and needs to be checked out. And because computers can sometimes take a long time to process data, you may want another kind of beep to tell

the user that your program has finished its part of the task.

QBasic makes it easy to communicate with the user through sound. The BEEP and SOUND statements enable you to make a variety of tones for a variety of lengths on your computer speaker.

Making Music

Beyond simple beeps and tones, QBasic gives you an easy way to play music with the PLAY statement. Although this feature is limited by the fact that QBasic must play out of your computer speaker alone, music can add a great deal to the right program. Of course, an accounting program would probably be silly if it played a concerto during the copyright message, but a game or educational tool doesn't seem right without music.

Using Graphics

Graphics can make or break any presentation. Like sound, even simple graphics add an entirely different level of communication with the user. Graphics are visual, and visual information seems to make much more sense than written information alone.

QBasic has many facilities for drawing graphics on almost any computer and monitor. You can draw points, lines, circles, ellipses, and arcs. You can fill in objects to make them one solid color. All you need is a simple statement like `CIRCLE (159, 99), 20` to draw a circle. With graphics this easy, you have no excuse not to use them when you need them.

QBasic makes drawing objects even easier with a special graphics statement called `DRAW`. This statement takes programs called *turtle graphics* programs, which consist of simple commands like *move left*, *turn 30 degrees*, and *skip left*. Though formed by basic commands, you can use turtle graphics and `DRAW` to create complex drawings.

Have Fun...

This set of lessons should be enjoyable. Here is where you get to add all the "bells and whistles," literally, to your program. Try each lesson, and be sure to experiment with what you learn.

LESSON 50

Sound Off!

```
1 ──► BEEP: SLEEP 1
  ──► BEEP: SLEEP 1
  ──► BEEP: SLEEP 1 ◄──────────────────── 2
  ──► SOUND 1784, 36.2: SLEEP 1

                                           3
    DATA 17
    DATA 3, 5, 7, 8, 10, 12, 14, 15, 17
    DATA 15, 14, 12, 10, 8, 7, 5, 3

    FOR I% = 0 TO 3
        RESTORE
        READ K%
        FOR J% = 1 TO K%
            READ Note%
            Freq% = 440 * 2 ^ (I% + Note% / 12)
            SOUND Freq%, 9.1 ◄──────────── 4
        NEXT J%

        SLEEP 1
    NEXT I%
```

QBasic makes generating simple sounds on your computer speaker a snap.

Type this little program and start it up. It plays the C major scale at four different octaves. Not impressive music, but a neat trick nonetheless.

1 Countdown

BEEP is a simple statement that generates a short beep on your computer speaker. You can use beeps in any number of ways in your programs. For example, you might use BEEP to tell the user that the value he or she entered is invalid. You might even use BEEP to tell the user that some long calculation is about to begin or has finally finished.

Unfortunately, the BEEP statement is not very versatile. It always generates an 892-hertz (roughly an A note) beep that lasts for around half a second. One tone like this doesn't carry much information, though, because the same BEEP would pertain to errors, warnings, and attention getters.

QBasic has another sound-generating statement you will see shortly.

2 Slowdown

Sometimes you need to make your programs take a breather. Even slow computers process things more quickly than humans can perceive, so you need a way to make the computer wait for its human master. In an earlier Part you used the SLEEP statement to make QBasic wait for the user to press any key. You can use SLEEP in another way.

If you give SLEEP an argument, like SLEEP 30, QBasic suspends your program for the number of seconds you indicate. SLEEP 60 makes the program wait for one minute, then it wakes up and goes about the business you programmed it to do. Even if you give SLEEP a time limit, it still wakes your program up if the user strikes any key.

3 More Than Just a BEEP

The other statement that QBasic gives you for generating sound is, appropriately enough, the SOUND statement. SOUND enables you to indicate a frequency and a duration for the sound you want to come out of your computer speaker. The frequency is measured in hertz, but duration is measured in an odd unit called ticks. There are 18.2 *ticks* per second. So, for example, to make QBasic play the middle A note for 1.5 seconds, you type the statement SOUND 440, 27.3.

4 What SOUND Can Do

QBasic enables you to generate many different sounds with the SOUND statement. You can use frequencies between 37 hertz and 32,767 hertz. If you use frequencies larger than 32,767 hertz you get an Overflow Error from QBasic.

You also can specify a duration between 0 and 65,535 ticks, although you probably do not want to generate any particular sound for one full hour!

WHAT DOES IT MEAN?

Your computer hardware stops whatever it is doing 18.2 times a second to take care of itself; it stops disk drives that are not being used, it updates the keyboard lights, etc. Each interruption is counted as a *tick*.

LESSON 51

Making Music

```
        ' A little Toccata & Fugue
3  →    PLAY "T255"  ' set the number of quarter notes per
                       minute
4  →    PLAY "ML"    ' music should be played legato

        PLAY "<L8 AG# L2 A P2 L8 GFED L2 C# L1 D P1"
2  →    PLAY "<L8 AG# L2 A P2 EF L2 C# L1 D P1"
        PLAY "<L8 AG# L2 A P2 L8 GFED L2 C# L1 D P1"
5  →    PLAY "L2 C#EGB- >C# L1 E P4 L4 GE L2 F#"
```

1

6

BEEP and SOUND are useful statements for generating informative sounds. You can generate different sounds for errors, warnings, or attention getters. The sample program in Lesson 50 used SOUND to generate simple music. QBasic has a much more sophisticated way of playing music than with the SOUND statement. Try this:

1 Making Music with PLAY

If you really want to put a little music into your programs, using the SOUND statement is probably not the way. With the PLAY statement, QBasic enables you to make some fairly sophisticated music. QBasic does not have multiple voices or instrumentation, but the music you can generate is still quite exciting! And even if you don't know much about music theory, you can still have fun playing around with PLAY.

The PLAY statement uses strings to decide what to play. For example, PLAY "BAC" plays the notes B then A then C. QBasic even understands

accidental notes like C-sharp or B-flat, and if you want to make QBasic play them, you just put the #, +, or - after the note. For example, PLAY "C#D+" plays C-sharp then D-sharp, and PLAY "G-" plays G-flat.

2 Octaves

QBasic has three ways to change the octave in which it plays notes. QBasic can play notes in the PLAY statement in any one of seven octaves, numbered 0, 1, 2, ..., 6. You can tell QBasic to play the following notes at one of these particular octaves by putting something like O3 in the play string. O3 tells QBasic to play the notes at octave number 3.

The > and < characters make changing octaves even easier; < plays the notes at the next octave down, and > plays them at the next octave up.

3 Parameters

In QBasic, you can set many parameters that affect the way the notes are played. At this point in the program, for example, PLAY "T255" tells QBasic to set the tempo of the music to 255 quarter notes per minute. You can set the tempo to any value between 32 and 255 the same way. Try setting the tempo much slower and run the program again.

WHY WORRY?

If you try to set one of the parameters to a value that QBasic does not accept, you get an `Illegal Function Call` error. For example, `PLAY "T 10"` gets you in trouble because you can set the tempo only between 32 and 255.

4 Technique

Use the PLAY statement to tell QBasic how to string the notes together when they are played. Normal music has small but perceptible breaks between each note. To make QBasic play normal music you can use PLAY "MN", or just put the characters MN in a longer play string.

When music is played legato, the notes are played with no break in between. QBasic can play music this way with the line PLAY "ML". One other style of playing music is called staccato. Staccato is much like the way QBasic plays music normally, but the breaks between each note are a little longer. You can make QBasic play notes staccato with PLAY "MS".

5 Note Length

One thing that makes music interesting is that notes can have different lengths. In common music, whole notes last for four beats, half notes for two, and quarter notes for one. The beat is set by the tempo, which you already know how to change.

To change the length of the notes that QBasic plays, you can insert something like L16 into a play string. L16 tells QBasic that the next set of notes is to be played like sixteenth notes. Sixteenth notes are played only one-fourth as long as quarter notes. Other ways to set the note length are PLAY "L1" for whole notes, L4 for quarter notes, and so on.

You can change the length of the notes anywhere in a play string, but only the notes that follow one of the strings like L8 are affected.

6 Rests

Insert rests into your play strings the same way you tell QBasic how long to play the next several notes. But rather than L, you use P for pause.

7 Experiment!

Use good judgment when putting music into your programs. An entire song probably would not fit well in a program that prints out checks, but a little three-note warning may be nice to warn of an overdraft account, an illegal value, or any number of things.

Reserved words   Identifiers and symbols   Strings and numbers   Comments

LESSON 52

Getting into Graphics

```
1 ───▶ CLS ' Clear the screen
2 ───▶ SCREEN 1 ' Get into 320x200 graphics, 4 colors
      PRINT "Hello, from graphics mode!"
      PRINT "Press any key..."

      SLEEP

3 ───▶ SCREEN 0 ' Return to text mode
```

Even basic graphics can jazz up almost any program. Fortunately, you can do graphics easily in QBasic. This program shows you how to get into and out of graphics mode with the SCREEN statement.

1 Clearing the Screen

Clearing the screen is always helpful; cluttered displays can confuse any user. The CLS statement erases the display and leaves you with a clean slate.

2 Switching Modes

QBasic has many modes. In the preceding lesson you read about the modes that control how QBasic plays music. QBasic also has modes that tell it how to display items to the screen. These modes are called *screen modes*.

When you start your programs in QBasic, you are operating in text mode, also called screen mode 0. In this screen mode, you can display only characters. Graphics are not allowed.

To generate graphics, you use the SCREEN statement to make QBasic switch into one of the graphics modes.

When you are ready to switch modes, put the SCREEN statement in your program with the screen mode number after the statement. For example, SCREEN 1 tells QBasic to switch to screen mode 1. In this mode, you can do graphics on a 320-by-200 grid with up to four different colors.

WHY WORRY?

If you try to set the screen mode to a graphics mode that your video card does not support, QBasic gives you an Illegal Function Call error.

3 Switching Back

You can always use the PRINT statement in any of the graphics modes to display text. But if you are done with graphics and want to go back to text mode, SCREEN 0 goes back to text mode and clears the screen.

4 Screen Modes and Resolutions

QBasic supports many different screen modes, but they all depend on what kind of video card you have installed in your computer. Screen mode 1 works on any video card that supports graphics, from CGA to WGA.

The rest of this Part uses only screen mode 1 because it is supported by most video cards.

LESSON 53

Plotting Points

```
SCREEN 1 ' Get into graphics mode                    1

10    FOR I% = 20 TO 40                               2
         PSET (20, I%)
         FOR J% = 1 TO 20 : PSET STEP (1, 0) :
         NEXT J%
      NEXT I%

      SLEEP 1                                         3

20    FOR I% = 20 TO 40                               4
         PRESET (20, I%)
         FOR J% = 1 TO 20 : PRESET STEP (1, 0):
         NEXT J%
      NEXT I%

      SLEEP 1 :  GO TO 10
```

Now that you know how to get into graphics mode, you can begin to draw.

Try this program. Read each numbered item carefully to see how to plot points. If you start this program, you need to use Ctrl-Break to stop it.

1 Coordinates

After you are in a graphics mode, you can use QBasic's graphics statements to draw elements, like points, lines, and circles. But how do you tell QBasic where to draw these graphics?

QBasic uses a pair of numbers called *coordinates* to locate graphics. Coordinates look like

(10, 20). The first number tells how far from the left side of the screen this point is located. The second number tells how far from the top. QBasic recognizes the top left corner of the screen as (0, 0), but just how far right and down you can go depends on the graphics mode you are in.

The programs in this Part use screen mode 1, which uses a 320-by-200 pixel screen. Each row of the screen has 320 points (or pixels), and each column has 200 points. So, for example, the point (319, 199) is the bottom right point, and (159, 99) is the exact center of the screen.

2 Turning Points On

The PSET statement tells QBasic to turn some point of the screen on. If you want to turn on the pixel in the center of the screen, you tell QBasic PSET (159, 99).

3 Turning Points Off

QBasic also has the statement PRESET, which turns pixels off. But like PSET, all that the PRESET statement does is change the color of a pixel to the background color.

PRESET also enables you to specify a color number along with the point that you want to turn off. So what is the difference between the statements PSET (25, 25), 3 and PRESET (25, 25), 3? There is no difference. Both statements set the color of the pixel at point (25, 25) to color number 3.

4 Relative Coordinates

Each time you tell QBasic to draw something, it remembers the last point that was drawn in the *graphics cursor*. If you put the keyword STEP immediately after PSET or PRESET, QBasic changes the color of the point relative to the graphics cursor. QBasic finds the point you indicate by starting at the graphics cursor rather than the top left corner of the screen. What pixel would turn on if you changed the second statement to PSET STEP (-5, -5)?

WHY WORRY?

Why is the extreme right point 319 from the left and not 320? Because the points are numbered starting at 0, the second column of the screen is really numbered 1, the third is numbered 2, and so on. For the same reason, the extreme bottom point is 199 from the top.

WHY WORRY?

PSET does not really turn points on or off but simply changes the color of the display at the point you give it. When you switch into graphics mode, QBasic sets all the pixels to the color of the background color. Using PSET just sets the color of a pixel to the current foreground color.

WHAT DOES IT MEAN?

Relative coordinates tell QBasic to find the point you indicate by moving down and left from the last point that was drawn rather than from the upper left corner of the screen. Relative coordinates have the keyword STEP in front to distinguish them from normal, or *absolute*, coordinates. You can use relative coordinates any place you use absolute coordinates.

Reserved words   Identifiers and symbols   Strings and numbers   Comments

LESSON 54

Geometric Figures

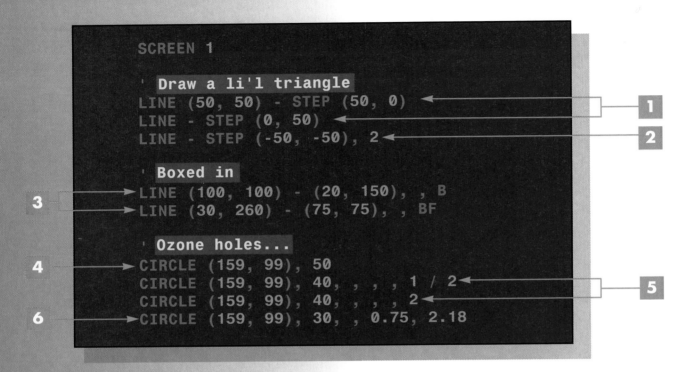

```
SCREEN 1

' Draw a li'l triangle
LINE (50, 50) - STEP (50, 0)          1
LINE - STEP (0, 50)
LINE - STEP (-50, -50), 2             2

' Boxed in
LINE (100, 100) - (20, 150), , B      3
LINE (30, 260) - (75, 75), , BF

' Ozone holes...
CIRCLE (159, 99), 50                  4
CIRCLE (159, 99), 40, , , , 1 / 2     5
CIRCLE (159, 99), 40, , , , 2
CIRCLE (159, 99), 30, , 0.75, 2.18    6
```

Plotting points is useful, but drawing figures like lines and circles is slow and tedious if you draw them point-by-point with your own program. The following program shows you how to use the LINE and CIRCLE statements:

1 Connect the Dots

When you want QBasic to draw a line between two points, you use the LINE statement. The LINE statement has many options. If you give two points to LINE, QBasic draws a line between those two points. For example, LINE (10, 10) - (50, 20) draws a line between points (10, 10) and (50, 20). If you leave off the first point, like with LINE - (10, 10), QBasic draws the line so

it connects the point marked by the graphics cursor with the point (10, 10). Playing connect the dots is a snap with LINE.

2 Colors

Just as with PSET and PRESET, you can tell QBasic to use a particular color number. If you leave the color number out, QBasic uses the foreground color.

3 Don't Box Me In

You can draw boxes by drawing four separate lines, and because you can leave the starting point off the LINE statement, connecting the corners is no problem. However, QBasic makes drawing boxes and squares much easier.

After indicating the color, you can type `, B` or `, BF` to tell QBasic to draw a square or a box (a filled square).

QBasic lets you omit the color number, so you can type `LINE (10, 10) - STEP (-5, 50), , BF` to draw a filled square with the upper left corner at the point `(10, 10)` and the lower right corner at the point `(5, 60)`. Try this example with different points and colors. Use `LINE` to draw a frame on the screen for all the gorgeous pictures you will draw!

4 Circles

QBasic's `CIRCLE` statement draws perfect circles for you.

To draw circles, you just give QBasic a statement like `CIRCLE (159, 99), 50`. The point tells QBasic where you want the center of the circle, and the next number tells QBasic the radius of your circle in pixels. You also can give `CIRCLE` a color number. With the `CIRCLE` statement, the color number comes after the radius, like with `CIRCLE (10, 10), 5, 2`.

5 Ellipses

The same statement that draws circles can draw ovals, or ellipses (a stretched circle). The amount of stretching is called the *aspect ratio*. You can give the `CIRCLE` statement an aspect ratio (other than 1) as the sixth argument to the function.

6 Arcs

You don't always need to draw full circles. Suppose that you are drawing a pie chart. To split a circle into the appropriate pieces, you may want QBasic to draw only a portion of the circle. To tell QBasic to draw only part of a circle or an ellipse, you give the statement a starting and ending angle, measured in radians.

WHAT DOES IT MEAN?

Radians are another way to measure angles. A full circle has 360° and 2π radians (where π is 3.141). Conversion between these measurements is easy. To get radians from degrees, you divide the angle by 360 and multiply by 2π. To get back to degrees, you multiply by 360 and divide by 2π.

WHAT DOES IT MEAN?

The aspect ratio is really the ratio of the lengths of the vertical and horizontal axes. For example, if you want an ellipse that is twice as long as it is wide, the aspect ratio you give the `CIRCLE` statement is 2, like this: `CIRCLE (159, 99), 50, , , , 2`. If you want an ellipse that is stretched the other way so it is twice as wide as it is long, you change this aspect ratio to 1/2.

LESSON 55

Filling Figures

```
SCREEN 1

LINE (10, 10) - STEP (20, 20), , B
PAINT (20, 20)

LINE (10, 35) - STEP (20, 20), 2, B
PAINT (20, 45), 1, 2
```

1

2

3

With the exception of filled squares, the figures you have learned to draw are like cookie cutters that stamp out a piece of the background. You can greatly enhance your images with the PAINT statement:

1 Painting with Solids

The easiest way to use the PAINT statement is to give it just one coordinate. This coordinate must be someplace within the area of the screen you want QBasic to fill with the current foreground color.

2 Borders

What is the area that QBasic fills? You can think of the PAINT command like a child with a coloring book. You point to a spot on the page that is surrounded by a border, and PAINT fills the entire figure formed by the border with one color. A border is just a series of pixels that have the same color and touch each other. For example, if you use LINE to draw a square, the square defines a border that PAINT can fill.

WHY WORRY?

When you use the PAINT statement to fill in the area of the display surrounded by a border, the border must be *closed*, or the PAINT statement fills the entire display with color. A border is closed as long as the pixels inside the border don't touch any pixels outside the border, even diagonally.

3 Setting the Limits

If you are going to fill in an area of the display, but the border you want does not have the current foreground color, you need to tell the PAINT command what color to look for. The second and third arguments you can give with the PAINT statement indicate the fill color and the border color.

LESSON 56

Turtle Graphics

```
                                                           7
    SCREEN 1
1 → DRAW "BM20,20 U10 L10 D10 R10"        ' Really square
2 → DRAW "BM40,20 E10 F10 G10 H10"        ' Cockeyed square
    DRAW "BM100,20 TA30 U10 TA150 U10 TA-90 U10 TA0"
3 → DRAW "C2 BM140,20 E10 F10 G10 H10"
5 → DRAW "S16 BM159,99 TA30 U10 TA150 U10 TA-90 U10 TA0 "
6                                                          4
```

By now you have seen many statements that simplify tasks in QBasic with strings. PRINT USING used format strings to enable you to format numbers and strings at output time. PLAY used play strings to tell QBasic what notes to play and how to play them. The DRAW statement does for drawing what these other statements do for output and sound.

1 Moving a Turtle

WHAT DOES IT MEAN?

The sequences of characters that make the DRAW statement work are called *turtle graphics*. Imagine a turtle with pens of various colors attached to its tail. Tell the turtle which way to move and how far to go. Dragging its tail with pens attached, the turtle draws lines of color on your screen.

The simplest things to tell a turtle are direction and distance. For example, you tell the turtle to go up 5 pixels with DRAW "U5". As the turtle moves, it changes the color of pixels, and so you get a line that is 5 pixels high. Likewise, you can use D5, L10, or R7 to make the turtle move down 5, left 10, or right 7 pixels. To make

things simpler, if you want the turtle to hop only one pixel in any direction, you don't need to give it a distance.

2 Diagonal Turtles

You are not stuck with the four cardinal directions: left, right, up, and down. The characters E, F, G, and H make the turtle move up and right, down and right, down and left, or up and left the number of pixels you tell it.

3 Quit Dragging Your Tail!

You can make the turtle move without drawing by putting the letter B right before the move command.

4 Turning

Turtles have heads, which means the graphics turtle faces a particular direction. When your program starts, the turtle is in the middle of the display, facing the top of the screen. As the turtle moves, it continues facing the same direction. This one-way direction severely limits the figures you can draw.

However, QBasic enables you to change the direction the turtle is headed by giving it a *turn angle*, like this: DRAW "TA45". After you indicate the turn angle, U, D, L, R, and all the other movement commands are rotated 45° west of north.

5 Scaling

If you want your image drawn at a larger scale, you need to tell the DRAW command to give you a new turtle with a larger tail. To request this change, you give a *scaling factor*. For example, DRAW "S4" draws images at normal scale, so DRAW "S16" draws them at four times the normal scale.

6 Different Strokes

You can change the color of the turtle's tail with the C command. For example, to use color number 2 you put C2 somewhere in your draw string. The color change affects only what is drawn next.

7 Mass Mover

When you want the turtle to be someplace at a particular time, you can use the M command. For example M10,50 moves the turtle directly to the point (10, 50). You can even give relative coordinates by putting + or - in front of either number. For example, DRAW "M10,-50" moves the turtle to the left 10 pixels and up 50 pixels.

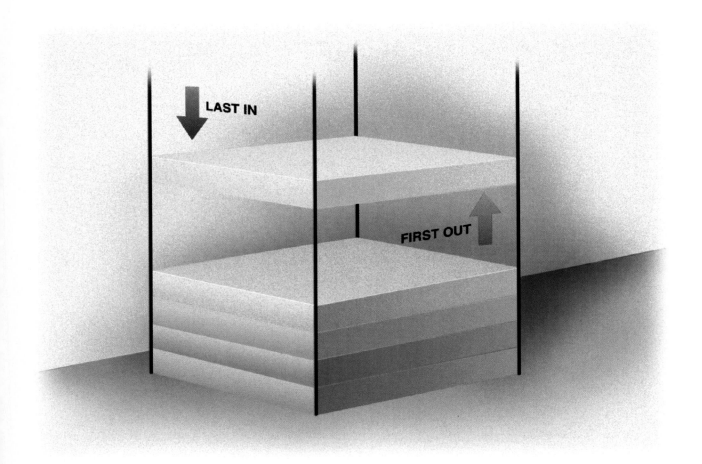

PART 9

Sequential File Input and Output

Up until now, you have learned various ways to input and process data from the user. Input has been from constants or DATA statements in your program or the variety of INPUT statements that QBasic provides. Getting input directly from the user at the keyboard lets your program adapt to the user and process information specific to his or her needs. But getting input this way can be extremely tedious, and you often need some way to let your program store information between each time your program is run.

Data files, stored in secondary media such as your hard disk, enable you to keep information that would be tedious or impossible to enter every time you run your program. Using files is not a difficult task. Read on, and with a little practice, you will be manipulating data files like a wizard!

57 Setting Up Your Files

58 Storing Data in a File

59 Retrieving Data from a File

60 Delimiting Data

61 Checking for the End

Filing Cabinets

The concepts you read about in this Part are probably not foreign to you. Data files stored in your computer are very much like files stored in a filing cabinet. In a filing cabinet, each file has a label of some sort and contains information. Some files contain instructions, like how the filing system works in the cabinet. Other files contain pure data, and these files in turn have scores of records on various items.

Computer data files are no different. Files in a computer have labels, called *file names*. The instruction files in a filing cabinet become *program files* in your computer. And just like data files you are familiar with, the data files in your computer contain various records. Each record contains fields for information like a person's name, address, and social security number.

The way that QBasic allows you to manipulate files mimics the technique you should already know. For example, to use a file, you use the OPEN statement. When you are done with a file, you must give the CLOSE statement. To read data from and write data to a file, you use statements you already know, INPUT and PRINT, with a slight modification to indicate that you are dealing with files.

Using files in your programs is not difficult, but you need to learn some details first. Let's take a look at them now.

Variable-Length and Fixed-Length Records

When records are stored in files in your computer, the way the fields are kept is very important. Records can be *variable-length* or *fixed-length*. Variable-length records contain variable-length fields. These fields shrink to fit the data they contain. On the other hand, fixed-length records contain fixed-length fields. When you write a program to use fixed-length records, you decide how wide to make the fields.

Suppose that you are keeping a record of a person's name, street address, city, state, and ZIP code. One such record belongs to Joe User, 203 Melody Drive, Lake Charles, IL, 77251.

If you store this record by using variable-length fields, 43 bytes are needed: 8 for `"Joe User"`, 16 for `"203 Melody Drive"`, and so on.

If you store this record by using fixed-length fields, you must first know how long each field is in order to size the fields large enough to hold the required information. You decide that the name field will contain 25 characters, the street address will contain 40 characters, the city will have 15 characters, the state will have 2 characters, and the ZIP code will have 5 characters. These choices are arbitrary, however. Using these lengths, *any* record would take a total of 87 characters, whether the record is about Joe User or Jane Doe. If you don't have enough characters to fill up one of the fields entirely, spaces take up the slack.

This figure shows the differences between these two storage formats. Variable-length records are covered in this Part.

Sequential and Random-Access Files

Besides the way that records are stored, QBasic has two methods to access the records contained in data files: *sequential* and *random-access*. Both methods have advantages and disadvantages. Sequential-access files are manipulated like an audio cassette tape. To get to a particular song on a cassette tape, you need to skip past all the songs before it. With sequential-access files, you must read all the data in the file up to the record that you want. If you are printing or searching records, this method is fine. But what if you want to delete or insert a record? To delete a record, you need to keep a temporary file that holds all the records you *don't* want to delete. After you have read the entire file, the temporary file becomes your new data file, without the

deleted record. As you can see, an operation such as deleting a record is lengthy and tedious. Sequential files may seem to be more trouble than they are worth.

But this assumption is not really the case. For one, sequential-access files are the only way to use variable-length records.

Because variable-length records do not use more disk space than they absolutely need, they are definitely the right choice when disk space is limited.

Many applications also lend themselves to a purely sequential process. If you are processing data and need to look at every record in a file, then a sequential file may be the right choice.

The lessons in this Part discuss sequential-access files. The next Part takes you through random-access files. Read carefully and experiment with the statements and concepts you learn here.

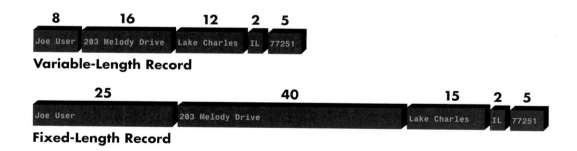

Variable-Length Record

Fixed-Length Record

LESSON 57

Setting Up Your Files

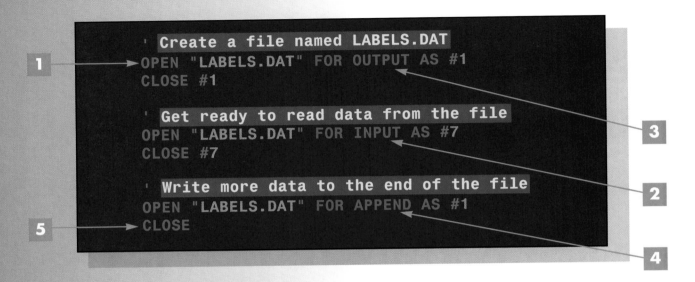

```
' Create a file named LABELS.DAT
OPEN "LABELS.DAT" FOR OUTPUT AS #1
CLOSE #1

' Get ready to read data from the file
OPEN "LABELS.DAT" FOR INPUT AS #7
CLOSE #7

' Write more data to the end of the file
OPEN "LABELS.DAT" FOR APPEND AS #1
CLOSE
```

1

3

2

5

4

Before you can read from or write to a data file, you must tell QBasic what you want to do with the file. In this lesson you learn how to tell QBasic to get a file ready to manipulate. With this program, you do not see anything on-screen. Take a look in your directory, though, and you will find a file called LABELS.DAT that the program created.

1 Opening a File

In the introduction to this Part you read about the similarity between paper files and computer files. When you want to access the files in a filing cabinet, you must open it first. In QBasic, you must do the same thing by using the OPEN statement. An OPEN statement has three necessary parts: a file name, a file number, and an access mode. The file name is a string constant or string variable that tells QBasic which file to open. The name can be any valid

DOS file name like "A:\LABELS.DAT" or a string variable containing a valid file name.

The *file number* is a number you give QBasic to use rather than the file name while you have the file open. A file number can be any number between 1 and 255, but you cannot open two files with the same file number.

WHY WORRY?

The pound symbol # before the file number in the sample line of code is optional with OPEN and CLOSE, but putting the symbol in is a good idea because it reminds you of the syntax of the PRINT # and INPUT #, which you will read about shortly.

2 INPUT Access Mode

When you open a file for INPUT with a statement like OPEN "LABELS.DAT" FOR INPUT AS #7, you are telling QBasic that you want it to get ready to read information from the file LABELS.DAT. In Lesson 60 you will learn how to read from files that are open FOR INPUT.

3 OUTPUT Access Mode

Before you can read information from a file, you need to create a file and put something in it to read. The way to create a file is with the FOR OUTPUT access mode. When you tell QBasic to open a file FOR OUTPUT, it creates a new file and gets ready to store information in the file.

4 APPEND Access Mode

The problem with the OUTPUT access mode is that it destroys any data that may have been in the file you OPEN. This problem greatly diminishes the usefulness of using files! But QBasic has another file access mode called APPEND. The APPEND mode is like the OUTPUT mode except that it does not destroy the data already in the file. Instead, QBasic prepares the file so that whatever information you put into the file is stored at the end of the original data.

5 Closing Files

When you are finished with a file, you should close it with the CLOSE statement. By itself, CLOSE closes all open files. If you want to be more selective, you can tell CLOSE the file numbers of the files to close.

6 RESET

Another way to close all open files is with the RESET statement. RESET takes no arguments but instead closes all files and devices that might have been opened. Because CLOSE does the same thing, it's a good idea to avoid the RESET statement. Using CLOSE by itself to close all open files makes your programs easier to read as well as prevents accidental closing of files and devices that might otherwise be required during the remainder of your code. CLOSE gives you a little more control over your program.

WHY WORRY?

Even though QBasic closes all files when your program finishes, it is still a good idea to close files when you are finished with them, especially files that have been opened for OUTPUT or APPEND. If a power failure occurs while a file is open, you may lose some of the data. Closing files ensures that all the data gets written to disk.

Reserved words   Identifiers and symbols   Strings and numbers   Comments

LESSON 58

Storing Data in a File

```
' Create a new LABELS.DAT file
OPEN "LABELS.DAT" FOR OUTPUT AS #3

' Use PRINT to store some data in the file
PRINT #3,          , TIME$
PRINT #3, USING "#####.##, "; 1000.50; 42.375; ↵
1320.2

' Close the file for now
CLOSE #3

' Reopen the file for appending
OPEN "LABELS.DAT" FOR APPEND AS #3

' Put some more information in the file
PRINT #3, "Doe, John"; "1412 Broadway St."; ↵
"Denver"; "CO"; 80201
PRINT #3, "Roberts, Robert"; "123 Elm St."; ↵
"Los Angeles"; "CA"; 90210

' All done for now
CLOSE #3
```

1
2
3
4
5

Now that you can get files open and ready to do what you want, you need a way to store data in the files. QBasic uses some old friends, PRINT and PRINT USING, to put data into files. The following program stores miscellaneous information in the file LABELS.DAT that the program in Lesson 60 will read back.

1 Opening a File

When you want to store data in a file, you need to tell QBasic to open a file so you can do so. If the file does not exist, the file should be created. This statement opens the file LABELS.DAT with the OUTPUT mode. This mode destroys the existing file LABELS.DAT, then creates a new LABELS.DAT for output.

2 Storing Information

In Part 3, you read about the PRINT statement that enabled you to write information to the screen. To write data to a file, you also can use the PRINT statement, with one twist: you must specify the file number. For example, PRINT #3, "Hello", "there!" writes the strings Hello and there! to the file opened with file number 3. The strings are stored in the file exactly as they would appear on-screen.

3 Formatting the Output

You also can use the PRINT USING statement as before to store information in a file. The only difference is that you must squeeze the file number in between the PRINT and USING keywords, like this: PRINT #3, USING "**$###,.##"; 1000.50.

4 Closing the File

Always remember to close any open files, especially the ones that have been opened for OUTPUT or APPEND.

5 Appending Data to the File

To store information in the file without destroying what was already there, you can open the file with the APPEND access mode. The remainder of this sample program appends a few more lines to the LABELS.DAT file created earlier in the program.

WHY WORRY?

If you attempt to write to an unopened file, QBasic will return the error Bad File Name or Number. Closing an unopened file has no resultant return error code.

Retrieving Data from a File

```
    ' Open the file
1   OPEN "LABELS.DAT" FOR INPUT AS #7

    ' Get the date and time
2   LINE INPUT #7, dt$
    PRINT dt$

    ' Get some numbers
3   INPUT #7, x, y, z
    PRINT x, y, z

    ' Read one character at a time until none are
    ' left
    DO
4       got$ = INPUT$(1, 7)
        PRINT got$;
    LOOP UNTIL EOF(7)
5
    ' Clean up
6   CLOSE #7
```

In the preceding lesson you read about a few ways to store data in a file. Now you need to get the data back into your program so you can process it. This program reads from the LABELS.DAT file created in the last lesson. The program uses several ways to read the file, so follow the explanations carefully.

1 Opening a File

The first step is always to open the file you want to use. This time, however, you must open the file with the INPUT access mode. You cannot change the data in a file if you open it for INPUT.

2 Retrieving an Entire Line

The LINE INPUT statement enables you to retrieve an entire line of input from the user, ignoring any special characters in the input. You also can use the LINE INPUT statement to retrieve data from a file by typing the file number after the INPUT keyword.

3 Retrieving Particular Data

LINE INPUT is useful for retrieving strings containing commas and other special characters from the user or from a file, but you bear the burden of deciphering the data. The INPUT statement enables you to fill in variables with input from the user without any hassle. INPUT also is a convenient way to retrieve data from a file. As with the other statements you have seen so far, you must tell QBasic which file the data is coming from by putting the file number after the statement.

4 Retrieving a Chunk of Input

Back in Part 3, you read about the INKEY$ function, which returns a single key that the user presses. A similar function, INPUT$, enables you to retrieve one or more characters from a file. For example, to retrieve 14 characters from file number 7, you use the statement INPUT$(14, 7).

5 End of File

This paragraph offers a sneak preview of the EOF function. EOF tells you when you have reached the end of a file. For example EOF(7) returns 0, or false, until you have read the last item in file number 7. After you have read the last item, EOF(7) returns -1, or true.

6 Closing the File

Although you do not risk losing data by forgetting to close a file that was open FOR INPUT, closing the file is still a good idea. DOS allows you to have only a few files, usually 20, open at any one time. If you leave too many files open, you may not be able to open any more.

Reserved words   Identifiers and symbols   Strings and numbers   Comments

LESSON 60

Delimiting Data

```
       ' Clear out the file
1      OPEN "LABELS.DAT" FOR OUTPUT AS #1
       CLOSE #1


       ' Store some addresses
2      OPEN "LABELS.DAT" FOR APPEND AS #1
3      WRITE #1, "123 Maple Way", "Los Angeles", "CA",
       90201, "Doe, John"
       WRITE #1, "4101 Maple Court", "Los Angeles", "CA",
       90201, "Roberts, Robert"
       CLOSE #1


       ' Get one of the labels (the third one)
       OPEN "LABELS.DAT" FOR INPUT AS #1
       ' Just ignore what gets read the first two times
       INPUT #1, label.address$, label.city$,
       label.state$, label.zipcode&, label.name$
4      ' Here's the one!
       INPUT #1, label.address$, label.city$,
       label.state$, label.zipcode&, label.name$
       PRINT label.name$
       PRINT label.address$
       PRINT label.city$; ", "; label.state$; SPC(2);
       PRINT USING "#####"; label.zipcode&


       ' Close that file!
       CLOSE #1
```

When running the programs in Lessons 59 and 60, did you notice that the names and addresses came out squeezed together on one line? This result is what you would expect because the PRINT statements that created this part of the file used semicolons to store the information.

Unfortunately, this format causes problems when you want to get the data back into your program. Where does the name end and the address begin? QBasic solves this problem with the WRITE statement.

1 Clearing Out a File

The first part of this program opens the file LABELS.DAT for OUTPUT then closes it immediately. This step destroys all the data that was originally in the file.

2 Storing Data

Remember that you should always close a file when you are finished with it. Try modifying this program so it asks the user to enter the names and addresses. Be sure that you OPEN the file only after the user has entered all the information and you CLOSE the file after the information has been written. A good idea is to always keep files closed while waiting for the user to input data.

3 Delimited File Output

The WRITE statement behaves like the PRINT statement. The difference is that WRITE puts double quotation marks around strings and separates each item with a comma. For example, WRITE #3, "bird", 7.0001, "cat" puts the line "bird",7.0001,"cat" in the file opened as file number 3.

4 Retrieving Data from the File

After you have written data to a file using WRITE, you can use INPUT to get the data back. You no longer need to worry about strings that contain commas. WRITE has enclosed strings in a part of double quotes. You also do not need to be concerned where one part of the data ends and another part begins. WRITE has separated each item by a comma.

> **WHY WORRY?**
>
> When you use WRITE to store data in a file, it is stored *raw*. You cannot format the data with TAB or SPC or even with format strings from PRINT USING. But the format that WRITE uses to store the data makes retrieving it from the file easy. Data files are only an intermediate way of storing information, so attractive formatting is not important. Users don't often look at their data files; your program is designed for that job.

Checking for the End

```
' Open the file for reading and look at the raw
' data
OPEN "LABELS.DAT" FOR INPUT AS #1        ◄── 2
DO
        LINE INPUT #1, raw.data$              ◄── 3
        PRINT raw.data$
LOOP UNTIL EOF(1)                        ◄── 4

' Reopen the file
CLOSE #1
OPEN "LABELS.DAT" FOR INPUT AS #1        ◄── 5

' Now look at the cooked data!
DO
        INPUT #1, label.address$, label.city$,
        label.state$
        INPUT #1, label.zipcode&, label.name$
        PRINT label.name$
        PRINT label.address$
        PRINT label.city$; ", "; label.state$; SPC(2);
        PRINT USING "#####"; label.zipcode&
LOOP UNTIL EOF(1)

' Close that file
CLOSE #1
```

1

2

3

4

5

6

As your program processes input from a file, it needs to know when it is finished. The EOF function returns a value that indicates whether the program has reached the end of a file. The following program uses the data file created in Lesson 61. It shows you the *raw* and *cooked* data from the file and uses EOF to know when to stop.

1 Raw or Cooked

When you store information in a file, it is usually stored in a *raw* format. All the niceties of spacing and numeric formatting are ignored. Only the minimal information required to get the data in and out of the file is used, such as commas and double quotation marks used by

WRITE. But after your program starts to process the data in a file, you generate *cooked*, or formatted, output.

You can see the differences between raw and cooked data in the preceding sample program. The first part shows you the raw data in the LABELS.DAT file, and the second part cooks the data for you.

2 Opening the File

As always, you must open the file before you can do anything with the data in it. In this example, you are only reading the information, so you open the file FOR INPUT.

3 Retrieving the Raw Data

This DO...LOOP UNTIL loop reads one line of the file at a time using LINE INPUT and shows you the line on-screen.

4 Knowing When to Stop

Because the file has an end, you cannot use LINE INPUT forever. At some point, you have read everything from the file and need to stop. The EOF function lets you know when you have finished with a file.

EOF takes a file number and returns True (-1) if the program has reached the end of that file. As long as you have data to read, EOF returns False (0).

Always check for the end-of-file when processing input. If you try to read information that does not exist, QBasic gives you an Input Past End of File error.

5 Reopening the File

After you reach the end of an input file, the only way to go back to the beginning is to close it and open it again.

6 Reading the Cooked Data

This part of the program reads that same data from the input file LABELS.DAT but processes it into meaningful, *cooked* output.

PART 10

Random-Access File Input and Output

Part 9 introduced you to basic file input and output with sequential data files. One advantage of sequential data files is that they can use variable-length records. However, by allowing variable-length records, sequential files are somewhat more difficult to use. To get to any particular record, you must start from the beginning of the file and look at every record, up to the record you want.

This Part teaches you about *random-access* data files. These files use fixed-length records, but you no longer have the difficulties associated with getting to a record in sequential files. Using random-access files is not difficult, and much of the information in the next few lessons should be familiar to you.

62 Setting Up Your Files

63 Describing Records

64 Storing Records

65 Retrieving Records

66 Positioning within the File

A Look Back

In Part 9 you read about sequential files with variable-length records. Variable-length records contain variable-length fields that can shrink to fit the data they contain. The primary advantage of variable-length records is that they don't take up any more space on the disk than what they need. However, in general, you can deal with variable-length records only with sequential file access.

Sequential file access is analogous to an audio cassette tape. To get to a particular song, you need to listen to or fast-forward over all the songs before you get to the one you want. Sometimes this sort of file processing is needed. But most other times, sequential processing is an annoyance. For example, if you are writing a program to manage an airline reservation database, you need immediate access to particular information. You have too much data to process the information sequentially.

Random-access file access is the answer to this problem. When you use random-access data files, you can go to a particular record of a file, without having to skip past or even see any other records. If you want the 1,025th record, you can read that record directly.

Random-access data files have a limitation, however. For you to skip around the records of a file, the records must have a fixed-length. Fixed-length records have fixed-length fields whose size is always constant. When you write your program, you decide how many characters to allow for each field of the record. Data that is too small is padded so it takes up the amount of space you give the field. Disastrously, data that is too large gets chopped off so it fits in the field! Nevertheless, the ability to move freely around your data greatly outweighs the disadvantage of fixed-length records.

Random-Access Files and Arrays

Earlier in this book you learned about arrays. An array is a group of variables of the same type, named by a single variable. To access a particular variable, or element, of an array, you need to specify the index number of the element. For example, if A% is an array of 10 integers, then A%(5) gives you the fifth integer variable in the array.

Random-access files operate in much the same way. Each record in the file is like an element of an array, and to access that record, you need to give QBasic the *record number*.

Accessing records with a record number is not difficult. In fact, you can think of record numbers as mailbox addresses numbered 1, 2, 3, and so on, all in a row. To get the information from some record into your program, you go to the mailbox with the number you requested and pull out the information. In QBasic, you use GET to accomplish this task.

Storing information is just as easy. However, the analogy of the mailboxes runs a little short here. To put information from your program into a record, you use the PUT statement. As before, you go to the mailbox with the appropriate number, but now, before you put your information in, you destroy any existing information. You may get into trouble if you try that step with real mailboxes!

Versatility

Random-access files open up many possibilities. If you experimented with sequential data files from the previous lessons and wrote your own programs, what you learn in the next few lessons should make your program simpler and more versatile.

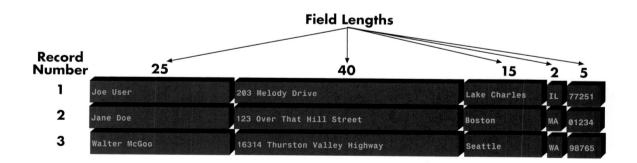

Record Number	Field Lengths				
	25	40	15	2	5
1	Joe User	203 Melody Drive	Lake Charles	IL	77251
2	Jane Doe	123 Over That Hill Street	Boston	MA	01234
3	Walter McGoo	16314 Thurston Valley Highway	Seattle	WA	98765

LESSON 62

Setting Up Your Files

```
   ' Open the file
1 →OPEN "INVENT.DAT" FOR RANDOM AS #1 LEN = 63 ←            3

4 →  ' Now close it...that's all for now
     CLOSE #1
                                                             2
```

In Lesson 58 you learned how to open data files for sequential access by using the OPEN statement. You also use the OPEN statement to open data files for random access, but many things are different. This program shows you the details of opening random-access data files:

1 Opening a File

You use the OPEN statement to set up your random-access data files in QBasic. As with sequential files, you must give a file name, an access mode, and a file number. However, random-access files always use fixed-length records, so you need to give QBasic a record length as well.

2 The Access Mode

The access mode used for random-access data files is FOR RANDOM. QBasic assumes that you are going to use random-access files, so if you give the statement OPEN "INVENT.DAT" AS #1 LEN = 63, QBasic opens the INVENT.DAT data file for random access.

3 The Record Length

To use random-access files, you must give QBasic a record length that tells the size of each record to be stored in the data file, without exception. The way to tell QBasic the record length is by putting LEN = 75, or whatever record length you need, at the end of the OPEN statement. The next few lessons show you an easy way to get the record length.

4 Closing Files

When you use sequential-access files, you should close files when you are finished with them. Closing files ensures that all the data is written to the disk. This point is just as true with random-access files. You use the CLOSE statement just like before; CLOSE by itself closes all open files, but you also can tell CLOSE which files to close by listing the file numbers after the statement, separating them by commas.

5 RESET

RESET works with random-access files as well as with sequential files. Even though QBasic does the same thing whether you use RESET or CLOSE, a good idea is to use the CLOSE statement to make your programs easier to understand. RESET takes no arguments but instead closes all files and devices that might have been opened. Using CLOSE by itself to close all open files makes your programs easier to read as well as prevents accidental closing of files and devices that might otherwise be required during the remainder of your code. CLOSE gives you a little more control over your program.

> **WHY WORRY?**
>
> You need LEN = when you give a record length to the OPEN statement. For example, OPEN "INVENT.DAT" AS #1 63 is not a valid way to tell QBasic to open INVENT.DAT with 63-character records.

Reserved words   Identifiers and symbols   Strings and numbers   Comments

Describing Records

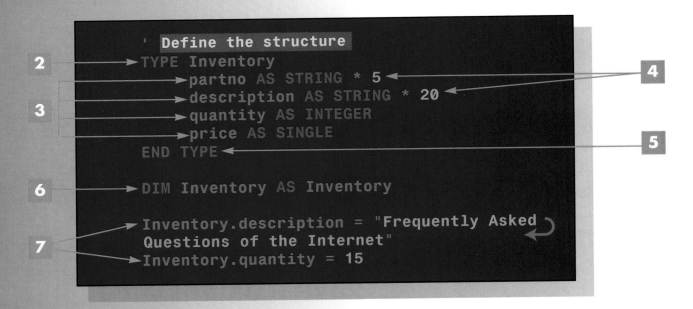

```
' Define the structure
TYPE Inventory
    partno AS STRING * 5
    description AS STRING * 20
    quantity AS INTEGER
    price AS SINGLE
END TYPE

DIM Inventory AS Inventory

Inventory.description = "Frequently Asked
Questions of the Internet"
Inventory.quantity = 15
```

After you have opened a random-access file, you can tell QBasic what fields each record contains. If you are using random-access files to keep track of an inventory, for example, you can tell QBasic that each record has a part number, description, price, and quantity.

The next sample program shows you two ways to describe the fields in a record:

1 Deciding What Fields to Keep

The most important part of keeping random-access files in QBasic is deciding what fields you want and how long they should be. Sometimes the length of a field is obvious, such as a ZIP code field. Many times, however, the length of a field is impossible to decide. How many spaces should you allow for a person's last name? You could say 25, but you may encounter one person whose name is 26 characters long! With

variable-length records, field length was not a problem. With fixed-length records, however, you must make a definite decision about the field length.

2 Defining a Structure

Structures are at the heart of using random-access files. TYPE...END TYPE enables you to define a type that QBasic can give to variables, just like integer or single. You saw this construction in Lesson 12, but let's take another look at it.

To define a new type in QBasic, you begin with a line like TYPE Inventory. This line tells QBasic that you are defining the new type *Inventory*. You can use any legal variable name for a type as long as it does not have a period in it. For example, TYPE MyRecord is valid, but TYPE My.Record is not.

3 Specifying the Fields

After the first line of the type definition, you indicate each field that you want the structure to contain. The field has a name and a type, such as `quantity AS INTEGER`. The `AS` keyword tells QBasic that the quantity field will hold only integer types.

You can declare a field to be any type, including other types that you have already defined. However, QBasic does not let you declare a field to be the same type as the record you are defining.

4 String Fields

When you define a type in QBasic, you cannot use strings as you have seen before. A type has a fixed-length. If you could use dynamic, or variable-length, strings, then the size of a type could change. To use a string field, you must fix the length of the string by typing the length after the keywords `STRING *`. For example, if `description` is a string field with at most 40 characters in it, you would use the line `description AS STRING * 40` in your type definition.

5 Finishing the Definition

After you have finished telling QBasic what fields to include in your type, you use the `END TYPE` statement to tell QBasic you are done.

6 Using the Type

Now that you have defined your type, you can use it in your programs. To give your type to a variable, you need to use a special form of the `DIM` statement. `DIM MyVariable AS Inventory` tells QBasic that the variable `MyVariable` should be of type *Inventory*.

7 Accessing Fields

To access the fields of a variable that you have dimensioned with one of your own types, you put a period after the variable name and then type the field name. If `MyVariable` was dimensioned with `DIM_MyVariable AS Inventory`, then `MyVariable.quantity` is the quantity field of the `MyVariable` variable, and you can use `MyVariable.quantity` just as you would any other variable.

Reserved words   Identifiers and symbols   Strings and numbers   Comments

LESSON 64

Storing Records

```
' Define the structure
TYPE Inventory
    partno AS STRING * 5
    description AS STRING * 20
    quantity AS INTEGER
    price AS SINGLE
END TYPE

DIM Inventory AS Inventory

' Open the file
OPEN "INVENT.DAT" FOR RANDOM AS #1 LEN =
LEN(Inventory)

' Store some data in the file
FOR I% = 2 TO 3
        READ Inventory.partno,
Inventory.description
    READ Inventory.price, Inventory.quantity
    PUT #1, , Inventory
NEXT I%

' Close the file
CLOSE #1

DATA "GBH00", "green broom handle", 125.32, 3
DATA "BRP00", "big rusty pot", 6.99, 97
DATA "BNW00", "brand new widget", 0.25, 1001
```

Now that you can create fixed-length records and random-access data files, it's time to put these elements together and store some data in your file. Random-access files use the PUT statement to store data from your program.

The following program uses the record you created in the preceding lesson to store inventory information in INVENT.DAT:

1 Defining the Structure

This part of the program defines the `Inventory` structure and dimensions the variable `Inventory` to be of this type. QBasic does not mind if you mix the names of the types you create and the names of variables.

2 Opening the File

Look over this line of the program carefully. You have already seen the `OPEN` statement for random-access files. However, this line uses the `LEN` function to make calculating the record length easy. In the first part of this program, you dimensioned the `Inventory` variable to be of type `Inventory`. Because `LEN` returns the number of characters that a variable takes up, `LEN(Inventory)` is just the record size you need for this file.

3 Storing Data

The `PUT` statement enables you to store a variable in a random-access file. To use the statement, you need to give the file number in which to store the record, a record number, and the variable that holds the data to be stored. The record number is what gives random-access files their power. Instead of storing each record immediately after the one you just stored (as with sequential files), you can tell QBasic to put the record in different locations of the file.

4 Storing Data Sequentially

Random-access files are based on sequential files. So if you want to store data sequentially, you can do so by leaving out the record number. Each time QBasic evaluates a `PUT` statement without a record number, such as `PUT #10, , Inventory`, it stores the record immediately after the last record that was read or written.

5 Closing the File

You are finished for now, so you can close the file. When QBasic reaches the end of a program, it closes all open files anyway. Nevertheless, closing files explicitly is a good habit.

WHY WORRY?

Record numbers start at 1 and have the range of long integers, up to 2,147,483,647 records given enough disk space. You can use any record number within this range for the `PUT` statement. Even if you have written only three records at record numbers 1, 2, and 3, you can still store a record at record number 10,001 if necessary.

WHY WORRY?

If you leave the record number out, you must still put a comma on the line as if you had a record number. QBasic gives you a `Type Mismatch` error if you omit the comma in most cases.

Reserved words   Identifiers and symbols   Strings and numbers   Comments

LESSON 65

Retrieving Records

```
' Define the structure
TYPE Inventory
    partno AS STRING * 5
    description AS STRING * 20
    quantity AS INTEGER
    price AS SINGLE
END TYPE

DIM Inventory AS Inventory

' Open the file
OPEN "INVENT.DAT" FOR RANDOM AS #1 LEN =
LEN(Inventory)

PRINT "Part"; TAB(7); "Description"; TAB(29);
"Price"; TAB(40); "Quantity"

' Get all 3 records from the file
GET #1, 1, Inventory
FOR I% = 1 TO 3
    PRINT Inventory.partno; TAB(7);
    ' Clip off some of this string...
    PRINT LEFT$(Inventory.description, 20); TAB(29);
    PRINT USING "$$###,.##"; Inventory.price;
    PRINT TAB(40); Inventory.quantity
    GET #1, , Inventory
NEXT I%

' Close the file
CLOSE #1
```

The following program enables you to experiment with the GET statement for retrieving records from a random-access file. Be sure to run the program from Lesson 65 because

the following program uses the INVENT.DAT file that the preceding program creates.

1 Defining the Structure

This part of the program again defines the Inventory structure and dimensions the variable Inventory to be of this type. You must use the same record structure for the records that you read and write to a random-access file. The order and type of each field in a record is very important. If you change the structure, you cannot read the data you have written to the random-access file.

2 Opening the File

Just like the program in Lesson 65, the OPEN statement here opens the file INVENT.DAT for random access. Notice that when you open a file for random access, you do not specify whether you are going to read from or write to the file like you did with sequential files. After you open a random-access data file, you can read from it and write to it without having to close and reopen the file with a different mode.

3 Retrieving Data

The GET statement has the same format as the PUT statement, but it does exactly the opposite. With GET, you give QBasic a file number, a record number, and a variable to store the data. The record number can be any value between 1 and 2,147,483,647. If the record you want exists, QBasic copies the data from the file on disk into the variable. However, if you ask for a record that is beyond the end of the file, QBasic fills the variable with blanks; all string fields become empty strings and all numeric fields become 0.

4 Formatting the Output

Remember that the information your program needs is stored in a raw format in data files. Your program processes the input and produces meaningful, understandable output. These few lines format the data from the file in a readable way.

5 Retrieving Data Sequentially

You can choose to leave the record number blank with the GET statement.

6 Closing the File

Your program is done with the file, so you should close the file.

Reserved words   Identifiers and symbols   Strings and numbers   Comments

LESSON 66

Positioning within the File

```
' Define the structure
TYPE Junk
    partno AS STRING * 5
    description AS STRING * 20
    quantity AS INTEGER
    price AS SINGLE
END TYPE

DIM Junk AS Junk
OPEN "INVENT.DAT" FOR RANDOM AS #1 LEN = LEN(Junk)

' Find the number of records
NumRecs% = LOF(1) / LEN(Junk)

PRINT "Record"; TAB(5);
PRINT "Part"; TAB(12); "Description"; TAB(34);
"Price"; TAB(45); "Quantity"

' Get all 3 records from the file, backwards!
FOR I% = NumRecs% TO 1 STEP -1
    GET #1, I%, Junk
    PRINT LOC(1); TAB(5); Junk.partno; TAB(12);
    ' Clip off some of this string...
    PRINT LEFT$(Junk.description, 20); TAB(34);
    PRINT USING "$$###,.##"; Junk.price; TAB(45);
    Junk.quantity
NEXT I%

' Close the file
CLOSE #1
```

1
2
3
4
5
6

This lesson covers some miscellaneous functions for finding out where you are in a random-access file and determining how many records have been stored.

1 Defining the Structure

As always, you must define the structure of the records you will be using for random-access files. This time, however, different names are used for the record name and the fields. Names do not matter when you are dealing with random-access files, only the type and order of the fields.

2 Opening the File

The OPEN statement here reflects the few changes that were made. The record length is what is important when opening random-access files, but because the Junk variable has the same size as the Inventory variable you used in earlier lessons, you should have no problems here.

3 Finding the Number of Records

The LOF function, length of file, returns the number of characters that an open random-access file contains. Because random-access files use fixed-length records, the size of the files are always multiples of the record size. All you need to do is divide the length of the file by the record size to find the number of records that the file contains.

4 Displaying the Records Backward

This part of the program uses the trick described in the preceding paragraph to display the records of the file, but backward. This procedure is not easy to do with sequential files, but because you can give the GET statement a record number, displaying records backward is trivial with random-access files.

5 Finding Where You Are

If you need to know what record number was just read or written, you can use the LOC function. For example, LOC(1) returns the record number that was last read or written from file number 1. Unlike LOF, however, LOC returns the record number, not the number of bytes.

One use for LOC is updating a file. Suppose that you use the statement GET #1, RecNum%, Variable to retrieve a record. If your program modifies the record and wants to update the information, you can use PUT #1, LOC(1), Variable just as well as PUT #1, RecNum%, Variable.

6 Closing the File

You have reached the end of the program, so you can close the file.

Reserved words   Identifiers and symbols   Strings and numbers   Comments

Index

A

ABS function, 115
absolute coordinates, 141
absolute values, 115
accessing fields, 169
addition, 99-101
APPEND access mode (files), 153
arcs, 143
arguments, 5, 13, 93
arrays, 21, 32-33
ASC function, 49, 125
ASCII tables, 124-125
assignment statements, 11, 21, 25

B

BEEP statements, 134
block functions, 90-91
block statements, 13
Boolean algebra, 58, 64-65
branching, 59
    conditional, 62-63, 66-71
    ELSEIF keyword, 69
    on variable values, 84-85
    unconditional, 60-61

C

calculations versus expressions, 96
calling
    routines, 80
    subroutines, 87
character codes, 124-125
characters
    converting strings, 128
    copying, 129
CHR$ function, 55, 125
CIRCLE statements, 143
clearing screens, 138

CLOSE statements, 153, 167
closing files, 153, 167
CLS statements, 138
columns (output), 46-47
comments, 7-8
comparison operators, 14
concatenation, 117, 120-121
conditional branching, 59, 62-63, 66-71
conditional execution, 6
constants, 6, 10-11, 20
    see also string constants
Continue command (Run menu), 77
converting character case, 128
cooked data, 161
coordinates (graphics), 140-141
copying characters, 129
counters, 59

D

DATA statements, 39, 50-53
data types, 6, 20, 23
DATE$ function, 126-127
decision making, 57-58
DEF FN statements, 88-91
degrees, 143
delimiting data, 158-159
describing records, 168-169
DIM statements, 23, 26-29, 32-33, 169
displaying
    fractions, 45
    variables, 23
division, 98, 108-109
DO UNTIL statements, 75
DO...LOOP loops, 74-75
double-precision numbers, 26-27
DRAW statements, 146-147
dynamic strings, 30-31

E

ellipses, 143
ELSEIF keyword, 69
empty strings, 121
END procedure, 77
END TYPE statements, 169

ending subroutines, 83
EOF function, 157, 160-161
exiting loops, 75
explicit data types, 23
exponentiation, 106-107
exponentiation operator, 98
expressions, 15
    calculation comparison, 96
    macro expressions, 88
extracting string characters, 121

F

fields
    records, 169
    variables, 34-35
file numbers, 152
files, 150
    closing, 153, 167
    cooked data, 161
    delimiting data, 158-159
    describing records, 168-169
    EOF function, 160-161
    FOR RANDOM access mode, 166
    opening, 152, 166
    positioning in, 174-175
    random-access, 151
    raw data, 160-161
    reading, 156-157, 172-173
    records, 150, 164
    sequential, 151
    writing, 154-155, 170-171
filling figures, 144-145
financial output, 45
FIX function, 110
fixed-length records, 150, 164
fixed-length strings, 30-31
flat notes, 136
Fld$ function, 122-123
flow control statements, 6, 58
FOR RANDOM access mode (files), 166
FOR...NEXT loops, 72-73
formatted output, 44-45
formatting strings, 45
fractions, 45, 104-105
FUNCTION statements, 17

FUNCTION...END FUNCTION statements, 92-93
functions, 16-17, 80-81, 88-89
    ABS, 115
    ASC, 49, 125
    block functions, 90-91
    CHR$, 55, 125
    DATE$, 126-127
    definitions, 89
    EOF, 157, 160-161
    FIX, 110
    Fld$, 122-123
    illegal function calls, 121
    INPUT$, 157
    INSTR, 119, 122-123
    LCASE$, 128
    LEFT$, 118, 121
    LTRIM$, 128
    MID$, 118, 121
    RIGHT$, 118, 121
    RND, 97, 112-113
    RTRIM$, 128
    SGN, 114-115
    SPACE$, 129
    SPC, 46
    SQR, 115
    STR$, 119, 125-127
    STRING$, 129
    TAB, 47
    TIME$, 126-127
    UCASE$, 128-129
    VAL, 125-127

G-H

generating random numbers, 112-113
geometric figures, 142-143
GET statements, 172-173
GOSUB statements, 82-83
GOTO statements, 60-61
graphics, 133-139
    coordinates, 140-141
    filling figures, 144-145
    geometric figures, 142-143
    plotting points, 140-141
    scaling factor, 147
    turtle graphics, 133, 146-147
graphics cursor, 141

I

identifiers, 9-10
IF...THEN statements, 13, 67
IF...THEN...ELSE statements, 68-69
illegal function calls, 121
INKEY$ statements, 48-49
INPUT access mode (files), 152
INPUT statements, 12, 37, 40-43
INPUT$ function, 157
input/output, 37-39
    columns, 46-47
    DATA statements, 50-53
    formatted output, 44-45
    keyboard, 40-41
    printing, 54-55
    random-access files, 163-165
    READ statements, 50-53
    RESTORE statements, 52-53
    screen, 42-43
    sequential files, 149-151
    SLEEP statements, 48-49
INSTR function, 119, 122-123
INTEGER keyword, 29
integers, 25, 28-29
    division, 104-105
    naming, 28
internal documentation, 7
intrinsic types, 34-35

J-K

justifying strings, 129

keyboard input, 40-41
keywords, 9

L

LCASE$ function, 128
LEFT$ function, 118, 121
LEN statements, 171
LET statements, 21, 24-25
LINE INPUT statements, 40-41, 157
line labels, 6, 9, 61
line numbers, 6, 9, 60
LINE statements, 142-143
LOC statements, 175

LOF statements, 175
logical operators, 14, 58, 65
long integers, 28-29
LONG keyword, 29
loops, 6, 59, 74-75
    counters, 59
    DO...LOOP, 74-75
    exiting, 75
    FOR...NEXT, 72-73
    nested loops, 73
    step size, 73
    WHILE...WEND, 74-75
lower case strings, 128-129
LPRINT statements, 39, 54-55
LPRINT USING statements, 54-55
LTRIM$ function, 128

M

macro expressions, 88
main routines, 80
math, 95
    absolute value, 115
    addition, 100-101
    exponentiation, 106-107
    fractions, 104-105
    multiplication, 102-103
    overflow, 101
    precedence, 96-99
    random numbers, 112-113
    remainders, 108-109
    rounding numbers, 110-111
    SGN function, 114-115
    square roots, 115
    subtraction, 100-101
mathematical operators, 14
MID$ function, 118, 121
MOD operator, 99, 108-109
multiplication, 98, 102-103
music, 132, 136-137

N

naming
    files, 152
    integers, 28
    variables, 26-27
nested loops, 73

Index

NOT operator, 65
notes (musical), 136-137
number conversion (strings), 119
numeric strings, 124-125

O

octaves, 136
ON...GOSUB statements, 84-85
ON...GOTO statements, 62-63
OPEN statements, 152, 166-167
opening files, 152, 166
operators
    changing precedence, 15
    comparison operators, 14
    exponentiation, 98
    expressions, 15
    logical operators, 14, 58, 65
    mathematical, 14
    MOD, 99, 108-109
    NOT, 65
    precedence, 15
    relational operators, 65
OUTPUT access mode (files), 153
output, *see* input/output
overflow
    addition/subtraction, 101
    rounding numbers, 111
Overflow errors, 11

P-Q

PAINT statements, 144-145
PLAY statements, 136-137
plotting points (screens), 140-141
positioning (files), 174-175
precedence
    math, 96-99
    operators, 15
PRESET statements, 141
PRINT statements, 5, 12-13, 38, 42, 138, 155
PRINT USING statements, 44, 155
printing, 54-55
    separators, 55
    strings, 129

procedures, 16-17
    END, 77
    see also subroutines
program flow, 58-59
programs, 5
    main routines, 80
    stopping, 76-77
    unreachable code, 77
prompt strings, 41
PSET statements, 141
PUT statements, 165, 170-171

R

radians, 143
random numbers, 97, 112-113
random-access files, 151
random-access input/output, 163-165
raw data, 160-161
READ statements, 39, 50-53
reading files, 156-157, 172-173
record numbers, 165, 171
records
    describing, 168-169
    fixed-length, 164
    positioning, 174-175
    types, 150
relational operators, 64-65
relative coordinates, 141
REM statements, 8
remainders (division), 99, 108-109
RESET statements, 167
RESTORE statements, 52-53
RIGHT$ function, 118, 121
RND function, 97, 112-113
rounding numbers, 110-111
routines, 80
RTRIM$ function, 128

S

scaling factor, 147
scientific notation, 11
screen modes, 138-139
screen output, 42-43
SCREEN statements, 138
screen clearing, 138

searching substrings in strings, 122-123
seeds, 112-113
SELECT CASE...END SELECT statements, 70-71
separators (printing), 55
sequential files, 151
sequential input/output, 149-151
SGN function, 114-115
sharp notes, 136
single-precision variables, 22
SLEEP statements, 48-49, 135
SOUND statements, 135
sounds, 132-135
SPACE$ function, 129
spaghetti code, 61
SPC function, 46
SQR function, 115
square roots, 115
standard division, 105
statements, 5, 12
    arguments, 13
    assignment statements, 21, 25
    BEEP, 134
    block statements, 13
    branching statements, 59
    CIRCLE, 143
    CLOSE, 153, 167
    CLS, 138
    DATA, 39, 50-53
    DEF FN, 88-91
    DIM, 23, 26-29, 32-33, 169
    DRAW, 146-147
    ELSEIF keyword, 69
    END TYPE, 169
    flow control statements, 6, 58
    FUNCTION, 17
    FUNCTION...END FUNCTION, 92-93
    GET, 172-173
    GOSUB, 82-83
    GOTO, 60-61
    IF...THEN, 13, 67
    IF...THEN...ELSE, 68-69
    INKEY$, 48-49
    INPUT, 12, 37, 40-41
    LEN, 171

LET, 21, 24-25
LINE, 142-143
LINE INPUT, 40-41, 157
LOC, 175
LOF, 175
LPRINT, 39, 54-55
LPRINT USING, 54-55
ON...GOSUB, 84-85
ON...GOTO, 62-63
OPEN, 152, 166-167
PAINT, 144-145
PLAY, 136-137
PRESET, 141
PRINT, 5, 12-13, 38, 42, 138, 155
PRINT USING, 44, 155
PSET, 141
PUT, 165, 170-171
READ, 39, 50-53
REM, 8
RESET, 167
RESTORE, 52-53
SCREEN, 138
SELECT CASE...END SELECT, 70-71
SLEEP, 48-49, 135
SOUND, 135
STOP, 77
SUB, 16
SUB...END SUB, 86-87
SYSTEM, 77
TYPE...END TYPE, 34, 168-169
WRITE, 158-159
STEP keyword, 141
step size, 73
STOP statements, 77
stopping programs, 76-77
STR$ function, 119, 125-127
string constants, 11
STRING keyword, 31
STRING$ function, 129
strings, 21
    concatenation, 117, 120-121
    converting, 119
    converting character case, 128
    dates, 126-127
    dynamic strings, 30-31
    empty strings, 121
    extracting characters, 121

    fixed-length, 30-31
    formatting, 45
    justifying, 129
    numeric, 124-125
    substrings, 118-119, 122-123
    times, 126-127
    trimming, 128
structured programming, 81
structures, 34
SUB statements, 16
SUB...END SUB statements, 86-87
subroutines, 6-7, 63, 80, 86-87
    calling, 87
    ending, 83
    GOSUB statements, 82-83
    see also procedures
substrings, 118-119, 122-123
subtraction, 99-101
switching screen modes, 138
symbols, 9
system date, 126-127
SYSTEM statements, 77

T

TAB function, 47
tables, 33
testing variables, 70
ticks, 135
TIME$ function, 126-127
trimming strings, 128
truncation, 110
truth values, 65
turtle graphics, 133, 146-147
TYPE...END TYPE statements, 34, 168-169

U

UCASE$ function, 128-129
unconditional branches, 59
unconditional branching, 60-61
unreachable code, 77
uppercase strings, 128-129

V

VAL function, 125-127
variable-length records, 150
variables, 6, 10-11, 20
    arrays, 21, 32-33
    character strings, 21
    dimensioning, 23
    displaying, 23
    double-precision numbers, 26-27
    fields, 34-35
    intrinsic types, 34-35
    LET statements, 24-25
    naming, 26-27
    single-precision type, 22
    structures, 34
    tables, 33
    testing, 70

W-Z

WHILE...WEND loops, 74-75
whole numbers, 28-29
WRITE statements, 158-159
writing files, 154-155, 170-171